This Is One Way to Dance

CRUX
THE GEORGIA SERIES IN
LITERARY NONFICTION

Valerie Boyd and John Griswold, *series editors*

SERIES ADVISORY BOARD
Dan Gunn
Pam Houston
Phillip Lopate
Dinty W. Moore
Lia Purpura
Patricia Smith
Ned Stuckey-French

This Is One Way to Dance

ESSAYS

❦

Sejal Shah

The University of Georgia Press ❦ Athens

Published by the University of Georgia Press
Athens, Georgia 30602
www.ugapress.org
© 2020 by Sejal Shah
All rights reserved
Designed by Erin Kirk
Set in Arno Pro

Excerpt from "The Site of Memory"
copyright © 2018 by Toni Morrison. Reprinted by
permission of ICM Partners.

Most University of Georgia Press titles are
available from popular e-book vendors.

Printed digitally

Library of Congress Cataloging-in-Publication Data
Names: Shah, Sejal, 1972– author.
Title: This is one way to dance : essays / Sejal Shah.
Description: Athens : The University of Georgia Press, 2020. | Series: Crux:
the Georgia series in literary nonfiction | Includes bibliographical references.
Identifiers: LCCN 2020001681 | ISBN 9780820357232 (paperback) |
ISBN 9780820357249 (epub)
Subjects: LCSH: Gujarati Americans—Biography. | Children of immigrants—
United States—Biography. | East Indian American women—Biography. |
Racially mixed people—United States—Biography. |
East Indian Americans—Ethnic identity.
Classification: LCC PS3619.H3483 Z46 2020 | DDC 8/8/.603 [B]—dc23
LC record available at https://lccn.loc.gov/2020001681

Title page image: photo of the author at age four,
with her grandmother, Indumati N. Shah,
who is looking through the glass door.

For R

♥

In memory of
LeeAnne Smith White
and my grandmother,
Indumati Natverlal Shah

Contents

Introduction

There was an intermission; it was that long. I saw *Gandhi* in the movie theater and still remember my indignation that the director chose a white actor to play the most famous Indian. Later I learned that Ben Kingsley is half-Gujarati; his birth name is Krishna. I was ten, growing up outside Rochester, New York, a part of western New York that's both racially and socioeconomically hypersegregated. I have always thought about race and representation. I wanted to see something of the life I knew in a book, on a screen. I felt that way in the long-ago movie theater as a child; I felt that way when I was in my twenties and in graduate school. Sometimes I still feel that way. I began writing to make a point of view, people, and entire cultural references I never saw reflected in what I read or watched.

This book is in part about growing up Indian outside of India, in non-Indian places; about the formation of ethnic identity in small cities and towns in the United States, away from urban centers. Kakali Bhattacharya writes, "We [South Asian Americans] are sometimes either invisible or hyper-visible, coopted by 'model minority' discourses or caricatured in characters like Apu in The Simpsons. Our invisibility stems from being racialized as non-white and non-Black, so that even in antiracist discourses we disappear because we are neither." I wanted to explore the feelings of both invisibility (of not even counting in the racial landscape) and hypervisibility (of always being other, a stranger, from somewhere else, the person expected to serve on the institutional diversity committee) for Asian Americans in this country. How do you make yourself visible and legible to yourself in a world that often does not see you or only sees race? How do you take up space? These essays meditate on objects and place. How do you move in a body often viewed as other? How do you claim the I, the person dancing, the person leading the dance?

Since my book spans two decades, and the United States and I have both changed in that time, I've noted the year(s) each was written at the end of the essay. In general, I ordered my essays chronologically by the present in each piece, though several move around in time. I wrote the earliest, "Skin," in 1999. Rereading and rethinking these essays has been a kind of excavation. I lived in picturesque Western Massachusetts then, a beautiful college town, and was frustrated with the lack of any visible South Asian or Asian American culture. I never felt as aware of being Indian and brown as during some of the time I lived in Amherst while in graduate school. During those years, the weddings of the kids of family friends, who were my friends from growing up, gave me a place to be unselfconsciously Indian, to dance, to connect.

These essays wrestle with identity, language, movement, family, place, and race. I am the daughter of Gujarati parents born in India and British East Africa. My life existed both as part of the diasporic culture in which I was raised (home, parents, community) and where I lived and grew up (western New York). I wrote these essays across twenty years, beginning in Massachusetts in the late 1990s and continuing through moves to New York City and Iowa, for fellowships and jobs, back to my hometown of Rochester. These essays address the passing of time, the loss of a dear friend, the childhood pool that no longer exists, my ambivalence about wedding jewelry, the brother-in-law I will never meet. I wrote about my older brother's wedding and ten years later, watching *Monsoon Wedding*. I wrote about 9/11. I wrote about what it feels like to lose a language you grew up with and to be able to express this loss only in another language.

I once called this book *Things People Say* after my essay "Things People Said" because I found myself so often incredulous and then furious over things people had said to me. It took time to unpack and unwind my visceral responses and what those words communicated to me. I could feel the kick underneath, the teeth. Microaggressions. Writing was a way to have my say—to pick up those words like a piece of glass and turn it over in the sun and consider the sharp edges or blunted corners. Telling the story, rendering a scene, making a list, allowed me to puzzle, to make a mosaic of these different parts. I believed there was something to learn and understand in my responses. However, I changed the title after I realized I didn't want to frame my writing only in response to other people's words. Why give them more space? I'll take that space.

Of my parents, brother, and myself, I am the only one of us who still lives in the country in which she was born. I have never visited the countries of my parents' birth with them, nor have I seen Uganda and Kenya at all. All I have is here. Weddings conjured those countries and cultures—theater, spectacle, acting, gathering. I think that's partly why they had a pull on me. For nearly all of the time I attended those weddings I was single. Weddings are about cultures and family and dancing. For me, they were not as much about getting married but about being young, about that time in my life, about having a place and a reason to dance. This is not a book about weddings, even though I write about them. This is a book with weddings as part of the landscape, and in many of those years I was in graduate school and a professor, I was a wedding-goer, hopping from job to fellowship to job, state to state, trying to make a life for myself. My friends and family did not elope. Weddings were family and community events. They belonged to more than just the people getting married.

♥

I don't subscribe to the notion of fixed genres—not when I and others move from one culture to another, from one kind of dance to another; from what looks like a poem to what looks like an essay to what could be a story. The world wants to know where to place you, how to classify you. I began my writing life as a poet, and later turned to prose. In the last several years, for me creative nonfiction has encompassed the wildest field of voice, thought, and performance. I view the essay as hybrid and nonbinary, the aesthetic as queer. Lyric or braided, traditional or flash, essays have granted me space to stretch, pivot, and grow. To meditate, ruminate, and weave. At heart, I'm interested in self-definition and invention. I worry the boundaries and borders to observe where sparks arise: they look like fireflies. We occupy space. I spin and twirl. I dwell and revel in the spaces between.

Prelude

[ ]

સેજલ

I am trying to describe what it feels like //
there is nothing but space in these words

;;

when language fractures in your attempt to speak //
when you are trying to talk back

;;

Here is my booth at the carnival.
        What will stay, and what will go: Indian, American, and girl.
        The body; bones, raced, erased.

;;

Stories are an argument between some words.

સેજલ

Weddings are a circle of stories, are bodies, streets, intersections.
        This is the body, dancing.

[I am a triple threat]

;;

My mother speaks to me in Gujarati. (My father in the other room, reading.)
These two words were once linked by a hyphen:
_____ - _____ .

But that is not the answer. I answer her, usually, in English.

the space   blooming   now   breaking   now
[there is no answer; there is only a door]

is widening now

[(I, too, call myself I)]

સેજલ

words are surfacing, one way to dance

[2002, 2019]

1

Skin

This is what the white boys say: Your hair. Your skin. This is what the black boys say: We together, together. This is what the Asian boys say: You date out too, I can tell. This is what the Jamaican boys say: I never liked you Indians. This is what the desis say: Get out of Massachusetts. Move to New York.

This is what the white boys say: But we would have brown children. And: Color doesn't matter. And: Why are you so obsessed with it. We're all Americans, right. How are we that different? My parents would love you. My older brother would want to go out with you. Your skin is your best feature.

This is what the black boys say: You got such nice eyes, girl. Your people have such big eyes. If you dressed hip-hop, you'd be my wife. We're almost the same. What is that dot, I like that dot. Never pay for a guy. What are you doing after. You saving it for your husband? Don't give it away to the white boys. Why not come home with me?

The brown boys are silent. I can't find them, can't see them at all. Sometimes there is a table of them, sitting on the far side of the blue wall. They talk and laugh in Hindi. We pass each other on the street, embarrassed. If we looked, we'd have to say hello. If we stopped to talk, if we went out for coffee, friends would say: Hey, when's the wedding, and: Oh, we love Indian food.

The brown boys, desis: They are too short after the white boys. You are too brown after their white girls. You look at each other helplessly. You are instant family, and then the instant passes.

Some of them remind you of your father when he was a student. He was thin then, wore the Third World mustache above his grin. How he looked in pictures: young.

This is what the brown girls say: Where are the good ones? There's no one here at all. We say: Let's go salsa dancing! Hit garba-dandiya raas. Let's go bhangra-hip-hop-reggae dancing: Springfield, Hartford, Manhattan, Queens! We are driving up and down Route 9, up and down 91, up and down Main Street.

We pass Emily Dickinson's house. Yeah, there was a woman who understood: Why even bother? Just stay in your house and write. We'll go to Net-IP next year. We'll think about going to India next year. We'll think about finding someone later. In the meantime: New York.

The problem with white boys is not just that they're white. That they would even think such things. The problem with black boys is not only that they're black. That they would constantly be trying to cop a feel. The problem with desis is not only that they remind you of your father and your uncles. The problem with Western Massachusetts is not just that you like this place. That you stand out in the snowy whiteness, that their mountains are really moderately sized hills, that this is where you live. That you are a brown girl here, never just a girl.

This is what they all say: You'll publish first. Hey Arundhati Roy, hey Jhumpa Lahiri, where's your best seller?

Here is a story about where you live.

Here is your best seller.

This is yet another story not about India.

[1999]

Matrimonials
A Triptych

1. KALEIDOSCOPE

I had never before seen people in my parents' generation dancing to Madonna, ABBA, and Kool and the Gang. They wore suits and saris; they flung their hands in the air. It all looked out of place, incongruous, dissonant. It was culture shock but also perfect: here was the moment I had been waiting for my whole life. I hadn't even known it could exist. All of us in one room, aunties and uncles and cousins and friends; Hindi songs and dandiya raas and New Order's "Bizarre Love Triangle"—a sonic embrace. When I think back to my brother and sister-in-law's wedding in 1992, it exists as one long moment in my memory: a swirl of skirts and sticks on the smooth wooden dance floor, my senses heightened by the deep jewel colors of wear-to-wedding saris—turquoise, fuchsia, purple, magenta—the high from hi-hello-kem-chos, bits of conversations in English and Gujarati with so many people from every part of my life; then words and colors and food, a five-tiered frosted cake, a kaleidoscopic blur of light and motion.

My brother married on a rainy afternoon in northern New Jersey. The mix of music at the evening reception—Hindi film music, American pop music, Gujarati dandiya music—mirrored the different parts of our cultural background in one setting. I had never seen anything resembling their ceremony and reception. Weddings join families and communities, spark joy, and suggest the possibility of cultures in balance with each other: a pure Indian Americanness I hadn't experienced in any other setting. It's an intersection I feel for a moment, before having to cross the street, return to my regular life, mostly in white America.

My brother's wedding was one of the first for the children of post-1965 Indian immigrants in the United States. The Immigration and Naturalization Act of 1965, also known as the Hart-Celler Act, abolished a discriminatory quota system that had been in place for decades and led to an increase in the population of South Asians in the United States. My father came to the United States on a student visa in 1967—an immigration history similar to that of many of my parents' friends.

The 375 guests included several of my more distant relatives who lived in and around New York City, and whom I had not seen in several years. At the time, my sister-in-law's mother had to convince the hotel to permit a small fire inside for the ceremony and allow outside catering (i.e., Indian food). I don't even remember the food—only the dancing. The wedding guests included relatives and Indian family friends and my brother and sister-in-law's friends from high school, college, and medical school.

I had never seen so many Americans (what we called anyone not Indian) dancing to Indian music. I had never imagined my brother's American friends attempting to play dandiya raas, a folk dance with wooden sticks native to Gujarat—and doing it pretty well. In raas, two concentric circles of people dance in a pattern—the inner circle travels in one direction and the outer moves in the other. Raas offers an opportunity to greet people you've known for years and to meet those you haven't yet met. In our other folk dance, garba, everyone forms a circle, moving right then left, changing direction, clapping then turning. Picture sea anemones washing first in toward the shore, then out, following the water, the graceful movement of a wave. Inside the circle is a smaller circle—the younger folks and avid dancers of any age bloom, spin, and turn faster here, showing off a bit, more complicated steps.

That June day in 1992 was one of the happiest in my life, Technicolor nearly. It was the first wedding for both families: my brother is the eldest grandchild on both sides, and my sister-in-law is the eldest on one side, the second eldest on the other. The occasion felt momentous, had weight. It rained that evening, but my strongest memory is of dancing—not the weather, nor that dinner was held up. It was the first time these separate cultures—Indian and American—and for me, distinct selves, coexisted, even merged, in one semipublic place. Hundreds of people dancing! The experiences of Indian Americans at this wedding, from the sheer number of people, the food, the music played, rendered our experiences, in Adrienne Rich's words, "real and normative";* the culture foregrounded was our own. This

---

* "When those who have power to name and to socially construct reality choose not to see you or hear you, whether you are dark-skinned, old, disabled, female, or speak with a different accent or dialect than theirs, when someone with the authority of a teacher, say, describes the world and you are not in it, there is a moment of psychic disequilibrium, as if you looked into a mirror and saw nothing. Yet you know you exist and others like you, that this is a game with mirrors. It takes some strength of soul—and not just individual strength, but collective understanding—to resist this void, this nonbeing, into which you are thrust and to stand up, demanding to be seen and heard. And to make yourself visible, to claim that your experience is just as real and normative as any other" (Adrienne Rich, "Invisibility in Academe").

was the first time I caught a glimpse of our faces in a larger cultural space. We were beautiful, multiple, mirrored, carnivalesque. We filled the room.

The dance floor welcomed everyone: the music spanned what we listened to on FM radio and what we listened to on weekend nights in a high school gym for Navaratri, the Hindi film music we also heard on the tape player, and the second language our parents spoke at home. To catch all of the references, you had to be Indian, you had to be Indian American—you had to be us. It was the first time in my life (outside of four incongruous weeks spent at Hindu Heritage Summer Camp in the Poconos) I didn't feel foreign or an outsider in the country in which I had been born and raised.

The DJ, a South Asian American named Mihir, called himself Magic Mike, and specialized in Indian weddings—he later deejayed several family friends' receptions. I'd never seen any evening glitter like this wedding—or been to such a large celebration other than Navaratri. Nothing that day exoticized or historicized Indian culture—it was not the India of James Bond's *Octopussy* or *Indiana Jones and the Temple of Doom*, or *Masterpiece Theatre*'s *The Jewel in the Crown*. It was not the historical biopic, *Gandhi*, released ten years earlier in 1982. We were right here, right now. The only thing that seemed over the top was a sleek ice sculpture of a swan: northern New Jersey took everything to a different level than western New York, even back then. The evening felt magical, a bright spectacle, larger than any life I'd seen. I didn't want the night to end.

The scripts for Indian weddings are established and standardized now: an entire industry caters to these celebrations. Hotels know that South Asian weddings are big business—often two or three days of events, an entire community invited and fed. Of course, there is no *one* "Indian wedding" or "South Asian wedding" (consider entirely different religions and significant regional and cultural differences), but there have been enough celebrations by now that those in the industry (and even some wedding-goers) know about the component parts of a Hindu ceremony: the tradition of having a sangeet or garba the night before the ceremony, whether or not a horse would be involved (as is customary in parts of North India, western India, and Pakistan) for the baraat, or groom's procession, the bride's mehndi party, and so on. When I married more than two decades later, David, the coordinator at the convention center in Rochester, knew more about Indian weddings than I did.

The Diwali Episode (2006)

My brother's wedding took place five years before DJ Rekha's Basement Bhangra dance nights launched on the Lower East Side and ten years before Bollywood films hit the mainstream, both profiled in the *New York Times*. Think back: no South Asian Americans on prime time or in the *New Yorker* or elected as governors of southern states. It was before we existed on screen or in the pages of a Pulitzer Prize–winning collection of stories about interpreters, maladies, and Bengalis in New England, an accepted and integral part of visible American culture. It was a different world then. It was before comedians Mindy Kaling, Hasan Minhaj, Hari Kondabolu, Aziz Ansari, and Kumail Nanjiani; before the Sri Lankan singer MIA; before the Diwali episode of *The Office*; before Jonathan on *30 Rock*; before an actual Indian doctor appeared on *ER*; before Obama celebrated Diwali in the

White House. In 1992, week after week, Americans watched Apu on *The Simpsons*, the Indian Kwik-E-Mart owner voiced in an exaggerated, stereotypical accent by Hank Azaria, a white actor. We watched *The Simpsons*, too.

If you judged by our representation on television and in books, we had mastered almost nothing in the public sphere. According to newspapers and the networks' nightly news, we didn't even exist yet. But we did. I did. Still, when I heard the reporters on NPR—Lakshmi Singh, Chitra Raghavan— every time I heard their voices and their names, I always stopped and looked up. I heard their voices and the nerves in the back of my neck constricted, attentive to the sound. I took notice every time.

Monsoon Wedding (2002)

Ten years after my brother's wedding, I watched another wedding unfold, bursting onscreen into petals and song. My friend Anita and I had gone to see Mira Nair's film *Monsoon Wedding*. Friends in New York had already seen it, so we had heard about it, but everything comes later to the provinces. We lived in Amherst, Massachusetts, graduate students at the University of Massachusetts. I remember it still as a bodily sensation, the visceral pull toward the screen I felt that day, when watching the film. I can still feel the electric current when I hear the music—effervescent—when I write this. I wanted to fall into that blazing color during the songs. Bright orange and yellow marigolds, red saris, pink turbans, the sky streaked with color, laundry fluttering outside. Although not a Bollywood movie, Nair's film acknowledged Bollywood's influence with multiple dramatic storylines, singing, and dancing.

Anita and I laughed without the rest of the audience joining in—we laughed at what seemed to be inside jokes for those of us who are Indian by birth or by affiliation, through diaspora. Neither of us grew up in India: Anita grew up in Papua New Guinea, and I grew up in western New York. We met in New England, hours from any major city. After watching *Monsoon Wedding*, we wanted to dance—we wanted someplace to unwind and expend the coiled energy built from listening to electronic dance music. But the only place I knew to go dancing on a Tuesday night was a salsa night at a local bar in Northampton. While I did do that often, that night a sadness surfaced, my wistfulness about the lack of spaces in which to simply be Indian in Amherst. I lived there for half of my twenties.

Weddings (1991–2011)

Throughout those years, I found those spaces during weekends of weddings—the weddings of family friends I'd known since I was a kid. For two decades, long weekends meant returning to Rochester for weddings; our Gujarati friends were our other cousins, our extended family. Through all these weekends, we celebrated how we had grown up in Rochester—the close community our parents forged—a parallel universe to the public schools in which we were one of only a handful of Indians. We saw each other on these wedding weekends: garba and raas on Friday, the ceremony Saturday morning followed by lunch—you have to feed your guests, of course. Nothing more important than food. Then home to nap and get ready to dress in a different sari or chuniya chori for the reception, dinner and speeches and all kinds of dancing. On Sundays, those of us who had come home for the weddings would meet for brunch before heading back to New York City, Madison, Albany, Hoboken, Atlanta, Pittsburgh, San Francisco, Boston, Cleveland, Detroit, Amherst, Washington, DC.

During those weekends, I felt such relief! My first trip to India took place when I was nineteen, a few months before my brother's wedding; I did not grow up going to India, and while a student and then a professor spent years in college towns hours away from a major city, or from any visible South Asian population. I cherished these gatherings and looked forward to when my childhood friends would unite and we could talk and dance together. On the dance floor, we could reach back to our younger years, revel in seeing each other and the launching of one or the other of us into a new stage of life.

I have always felt happy dancing. A few American friends have noted over the years that they can see something Indian in how I dance. Sometimes it seems as if one must perform one's Indianness for it to be seen and acknowledged. I didn't need my culture (diasporic, floating, race, language, food) to be acknowledged, but it does differ from those often around me, from those I am often around. And other times, later, race seemed only too inescapable: one will be expected to serve on the diversity committee for one's primarily white institution and therefore required to provide additional, invisible labor without compensation. I knew who I was during those years in graduate school, even if Indian culture wasn't around me. Still, dancing was an important part of how I understood myself to be Indian. It allowed me a space to interact with friends and strangers without speaking—no "Where are you from?" on the dance floor.

Come on Dance (2002, 2018)

While watching *Monsoon Wedding* in 2002, I felt engulfed by a nostalgia for an India I have never known, although I had attended many Indian weddings (Hindu-Hindu, Hindu-Christian, Sikh-Sikh, Hindu-Jain, Hindu-Muslim), mostly in the United States but also in India. The film created an almost palpable sense of how a wedding is a family event, a huge undertaking; how it (literally) filled the screen: the people coming and going, the costuming, the pageantry. I nodded at the bits of Hindi I understood, at tics and gestures I recognized as particularly Indian, desi, particular to Delhi and to Punjabis. The film centered on Delhi, Punjabi culture, and the ordinary reality of speaking more than one language. It did not see itself as foreign. The rest of the world existed (Australia, the United States), but we were off to the side. It showed the cosmopolitanism and multilingualism of India and also the presence of returned family from places like the United Kingdom. The movie also referenced common Bollywood tropes one can read only if familiar with the genre.

When I watched *Monsoon Wedding* again it was 2018, and I tried to understand why this film had seared itself into my memory. I remember that I listened to the soundtrack endlessly for a time, which for me meant listening to two songs on repeat. I even bought the CD as a present for each faculty member on my thesis committee; I wanted to convey some of what I attempted to create and represent in my writing—context, aesthetic, multiple languages. I tried to create a diasporic backdrop for my work, for how I hoped my writing might be read and situated.

On Facebook I asked, "Who remembers *Monsoon Wedding*?" Friends from all parts of my life weighed in, a stream of comments. It did mean something particular for those of us who are South Asian—many noted that. But friends of all backgrounds had something to say. It was a landmark film, both in how it presented Indian culture in India and in diaspora, and also in how well it did at the box office.

When I watched it again, I realized all that stayed with me is one song that kicks in with only eight minutes left in the film—the electronic music, the rain, pink turbans, ecstatic dancing—a kind of transcendence at the end of the film. Spirit rising! Imagine my surprise to learn "Aaja Nachle" ("Come on Dance!"), the song carrying the memory for me all these years, is such a small part of the film. By the time we hear the song, the plot has unfurled, the story line played out. I loved the exuberant, spontaneous dancing at the end of the film more than the whole rest of the film. Hindi words and then "Can you take me?" and the song does just that— it transports me even now back to the film, to the joy of wedding revelry.

Before *Monsoon Wedding*, the Indian character would have been a sidekick in a mainstream movie: the geek, the exotic girl, the older wise woman off to the side, advising the heroine but not equal to any screen time, a supporting character—a decoration for the stage set for other actors. In the final scene of *Monsoon Wedding*, it is the grandmothers who kick off the dancing, and then the young Indian guy arrives from Australia or the United Kingdom and he's walking in the rain; in another movie, he'd be cast as an IT stereotype, but here he is handsome, a hunk, a potential future love interest for one of the single characters. *Monsoon Wedding* and Nair's earlier film, *Mississippi Masala,* said to me, *Look: you can be a main character. You can take up space.*

I watched *Mississippi Masala* at a movie theater in Harvard Square a few months before my brother's wedding. Before this, I had never seen any representation of my family history (Indians in East Africa) on a large screen (or any screen) nor a South Asian American protagonist. The film follows the romance between Mira (actress Sarita Choudhury) and Demetrius (Denzel Washington's character) in Mississippi, where Mira's family eventually relocated after being forced to flee Uganda. Though I had my critiques of both the storyline and the stereotypes of Indian immigrant and black cultures, I also remember how liberating and extraordinary it felt to watch South Asian American and African American leads, their families, and stories centered in a mainstream film.

The desire to see one's self and community reflected runs deep.

2. MATRIMONIALS

I enrolled in graduate school in August 1997, which coincided with the fiftieth anniversary of India's independence from Britain. That year modern India arrived for America and its publishing houses, beginning with Arundhati Roy's lauded novel *The God of Small Things.* When India hit mainstream America, I found myself ambivalent. The private subculture of Indian Americanness I grew up as part of had reached the radars of both the *New York Times* and *Time.* It was time, yes. It was past time.

But which stories would be heralded and by whom? In 2002, the year I finished my degree, the headline of a lead article in the arts section of the *Boston Globe* read, "Nice to Meet You. Will You Marry Me?" Several people mentioned this article to me—about introductions or matrimonial personal ads, a modern twist on arranged marriages. Written by a South Asian American journalist, Anand Vaishnav, the article appeared soon after *Monsoon Wedding's* release. I read the story and wondered what non-Indian readers were going to think.

As a child, I remember my irritation when classmates or adults asked me about arranged marriages with an equal mix of horror and fascination splayed across their faces. Would I again be subject to comments about how strange it is to marry someone you don't know well, or the other kind of comments, about how nice it would be if an analogous option existed in this country for Americans who don't belong to a particular ethnic community? I braced myself against either kind of comment.

Perhaps my favorite part of the *Globe* article: the matrimonials taken from *India Today* and *India Abroad*, newspapers targeting the diasporic Indian community in the United States, also called NRIS (Non-Resident Indians):

Bengali Hindu parents looking for alliance from PhD/MD/ Lawyer, Under 30 in NY/Washington areas; for beautiful daughter; 25/5'4", CS/Econ MS, may pursue PhD.

Correspondence invited for Punjabi Hindu, 29/6'1", physician son, U.S. citizen, very handsome, cultured; prefers Engineering/Dentist/MBA/Pharmacist girl with family values.

As teenagers, my brother and I loved looking through these marriage classifieds in the back of the paper. We teased each other, finding ads that came uncomfortably close to matching our backgrounds, and laughed at the language, a particular Indian English we both recognized. I was both troubled and amused to see these ads appearing in the *Globe*. It meant we existed, reading these matrimonials out of context in the *Globe*, on the light-colored newsprint of an American daily instead of in the coarsely printed back pages of a newspaper I have not seen for years.

I look up recent listings from *India Abroad*, now online. The language persists, remarkably similar to what it was when my brother and I were young.

PHYSICIAN SON.

Handsome, very fair, athletic, MD doing fellowship in cardiology, 29, 5'7", U.S.-born, educated at top universities, raised with Indian values. Seeking MD girl, beautiful, responsible, good nature and family values. Email bio/photo XXXXXXX@gmail.com.

Details for Hindu South Indian Business family

Hindu South Indian Business family seeking educated/business professionals from USA/Abroad/India for never married medical doctor daughter 40s, issueless divorcees can respond; email: bio/photo: XXXXXXXXXXXXXXXXXXX@ gmail.com.

Master of Fine Arts (2002)

In the introduction to my master's thesis, I wondered, "Have I introduced my stories or am I introducing me? What if I wrote my own matrimonial? It's just writing a different introduction." I wrote,

Correspondence invited for 29-year-old 5'6" Hindu Gujarati (Nagar Vanya) slim, fair, writer girl; never married. Has MFA (not finance/administration; fine arts), like MS in English. Looking for professional boys, 30's. Caste no bar. Northeast/ California preferred.

Don't take it seriously.
My brother might laugh.
My brother might make suggestions.
We speak to each other almost always in English.

3 . TRANSLITERATION

After 9/11, my uncle sent me a T-shirt for my birthday, which falls in October. It reads, "Proud to Be American," the words embracing an American flag. I thought about using a permanent marker and circling the image. A circle with a slash through it. Or crossing out "proud" and marking "highly ambivalent." I talked to my uncle, and despite my hope to the contrary, he had sent the T-shirt in all seriousness. Did he think I would wear it? I didn't bother to ask. It was a shirt large enough to be a sleep shirt, anyway—not one I would wear outside. Then I noticed, after visiting my brother, that he had taped a computer-generated image of the American flag onto the rear window of his wife's car. My father told me that he dressed a little more sharply (shirt, tie, good shoes) when he flew in December. I had done the same thing when I flew in October. An American gas store owner, Balbir Singh Sodhi, was killed in Mesa, Arizona, a few days after 9/11 —in a racially and religiously motivated hate crime. His attacker wanted to retaliate against the Muslim terrorists. Sodhi was not Muslim. He wore a turban as many Sikhs do.

Understanding we are often read as foreign and therefore as a threat is another lived experience for many South Asians, Middle Easterners, and other brown-skinned people in the United States.

♥

I don't write in Gujarati, a language I spoke before I started school. Can you be Gujarati if you don't speak Gujarati? If you've only been to Gujarat twice? I can't access it in an easy way, the way I admire in Junot Díaz's stories, the Spanish words sitting next to the English. None of it explained.

♥

My grandfather, a labor activist, social worker, and (I learned after he had died) also an English teacher, taught my cousin and me three chapters of *The Bhagavad Gita*. Every day after school, we walked home with our red Tupperware lunch boxes, ate our snack, and our grandfather would teach us one verse or sloka. I remember somersaulting on the wine-colored carpet, trying to remember the verse. For us it was a game. Still, we learned over a hundred verses in Sanskrit. We never learned what most of the words meant. Even now, I can recite them. The cadence of this language that I do not speak in, do not think in, do not even understand, and which belongs to a culture that is mine, but not fully mine is part of what made me interested in language. At that time, our grandfather (Dada) transliterated the verses into English. Transliteration. Resignation. Regeneration.

In "Imaginary Homelands," the title essay of his book, Salman Rushdie writes, "To be an Indian writer in this society [British] is to face, every day, problems of definition. What does it mean to be 'Indian' outside India?" I have wondered about the answer for as long as I can remember.

In two separate years, I was invited to twelve weddings and attended six—a number of them Indian. The rituals of weddings engage us in a play of culture(s). How is culture performed and created in language? How can the English language be molded and modified to reflect the cultures that inhabit it, that it inhabits. For example, look at the word "desi," and its emergence in popular culture, in youth subculture, in art forms such as festivals and films. It is an insider/outsider term: one that has been claimed; one identified with a particular cultural, political, and progressive agenda. I love the title of Meera Syal's book *Life Isn't All Ha Ha Hee Hee* because of its Indian English bent, its particular flavor. The title, to me, is a reminder of how accommodating English can be of other tongues, even as I encounter its limitations.

❧

When my mother calls me, she speaks half in English, half in Gujarati.

❧

My father leaves messages on my voicemail in Gujarati. He forgets that it is not an answering machine and repeats my name several times, to see if I will pick up.

❧

One of my grandmothers learned to drive in this country. This means she took the written test. (Neither grandmother speaks much English.)

♥

In a poem about my mother I wrote, "The book she is reading lies open, but it is written in a language I cannot read."

Translation (1997–2002)

During those years in graduate school, the language changed. The culture changed. 9/11 happened, and what it meant to be brown in the United States changed. In all those years, I was never in a fiction workshop with another Asian American let alone Indian American. Nearly everyone was white. So much of learning to write in an MFA program meant translating, and that's just what I didn't want to do. That's what I resisted. Why must I give context for my characters? Who is my audience? Why should I explain myself to you? How do you make it through a program without giving another's point of view and references more weight than your own?

Weddings on those long weekends punctuated the long days and white spaces of graduate school and the academic year. They reminded me that there was a wider world out there—multilingual, vibrant, layered—every riotous color, each ephemeral dance. Just because it didn't exist in Western Massachusetts didn't mean it didn't exist.

[2002, 2019]

Who's Indian?

A South Asian friend of mine born in Guyana, raised in Canada, and living in England once said to me, "It always comes down to the same one question: 'Where do you come from?'" ... In time I began to see that it is actually the question, not the answer, which is problematic. Exclusionary and ultimately racist through its denial of self-definition, this question imposes criteria on its respondent: you must come from somewhere. Some *one* where that is most probably not from here.—JASBIR K. PUAR

A few days before leaving for a nine-day trip to Sicily, I met a young man in a bar in Northampton, Massachusetts, who asked me what my nationality was. I wanted to walk away from him.

"I'm American," I said.

He had the grace to look embarrassed. "But where are you from originally?"

"From Upstate New York," I said. Anticipating his next question, I launched into a version of my stock story: "My father was born in India, my mother was born in Uganda and grew up in Kenya. We're Indian; I'm Indian."

I felt I had earned the right to ask him the same question. When I asked him what he was, he answered, "American." So then I asked it: "But, where are you *from*?" He named a town in central Massachusetts. But before that? He was a quarter Sicilian.

The enthusiastic karaoke singers and crush of people made it impossible to have much more of a conversation. He was a nice enough guy trying to buy me a drink; still, I felt annoyed that the "Where are you from?" question was one I was expected to answer on a Friday night. I wanted what lots of people want at the end of the week—a chance to forget, to blur the edges a little, to be around some friendly faces; to lose myself in some music, in a drink, in an evening. To be a little anonymous in our small academic community. Not to have to explain who I am, where I come from, why my face looks different from the one who's asking the question.

❧

I think many of us travel for the same reason—to feel the edges of ourselves simultaneously sharpened and blurred. We are sharpened by the contrast of another language, a new place and culture, and softened by a willingness to see and be open to the possibilities of different selves while on vacation, in a time bounded by parentheses—by our inevitable return to the familiar.

My trip to Sicily was the travel component of a photo-journalism course I took at the University of Massachusetts, Amherst, in the spring of 2000. I had twice traveled to mainland Italy, and I loved how I felt there—how Italian sounded in my ears, how the Italians I met saw me as an American, how I didn't have to explain where I was from. At twenty-seven, explanations tired me.

❧

In Sicily, in the seaside village of Porticello, I dawdled, staring at the ocean, and lost sight of my classmates, who were eager to explore the area. I tried to stay calm. Some sidewalk vendors off to the side caught my eye, because one looked Indian. They stood waiting behind their tables of wares, at a flea market, not unlike what you might see on the main street of a small New England town, in the summer neighborhood festivals in Upstate New York, outside famous temples and ruins in India, at the weekend flea market in Park Slope. I strolled over and found myself at one of the tables.

Although drawn to traveling, I have always had an intense and irrational fear of getting lost, and this pushed me to seek out someone who could help me find my way, someone who maybe looked like home, someone who looked safe to ask. I grew up in a city where my family knew nearly all of the other South Asian families in town; these families formed an extended network of aunties and uncles, any of whom instantly and freely offered food, gathering places, admonishments, stories about back home, and rides to each other's houses to all of the children of the community.

At the row of tables, a man in his thirties or forties, with an open and welcoming countenance, smiled at me in an expectant, shopkeeperly way. A few feet behind him stood a woman who glanced up before returning to smoothing her daughter's hair. She wore a salwaar kameez—a marker of ethnicity, of origin. Many of my mother's saris and my chunidars quietly trumpeted that deep, prototypically Indian purple, and I knew the color would bleed—it was a hand-wash-only garment. She also wore a yellow-gold nose ring, to me a familiar sight and a welcome contrast to the thin silver nose rings ubiquitous in Northampton, land of the uniformly hip white girls.

I stood at the table, trying to say more than hello. The shopkeeper began to speak in Italian. Then he stopped.

"Indian?" I asked.

"Oh, Indian, si, si!" He nodded and smiled. "Parla italiano?"

"No," I replied sadly. "Parlo un po. Parla Gujarati?"

This is my language of regret—a language that I grew up speaking but now only barely retain; the language which, interspersed with English, signifies an intuitive recognition and marker of "home." I am a mute in Gujarati, easily comprehending everyday conversations but unable to wield phrases fluently, confidently, correctly.

He shook his head. "Hindi?"

I understood a few words, but not enough to carry a conversation or even fully understand. We discovered that the language we shared was English. Sokhi was his name, he told me.

Throughout all of this, I smiled at their little girl. Kids don't care what language you speak. My mother tells a story I've always loved, about my brother and a neighbor boy. Samir lived in India with our grandparents until he was three and a half, and didn't speak any English when he joined our parents in the United States. My mother says that the two small boys played together, chattering away. They understood each other, though each spoke only a language the other did not.

Although I was not entirely comfortable with the fancy camera I had borrowed from my sister-in-law for the trip, I decided it would be good to get a picture of this family, of these Indians outside India. I could envision using this photo for a final project, but more than that, the interaction was already shaping itself into an anecdote that I could imagine recollecting to my family and friends. It would be one more piece in that stash of what we collect when traveling: ticket stubs, postcards, the products of obsessive photo taking of moments and people that in my own neighborhood I noted only in passing and almost never recorded. This wanting: the desire to carry back something—a shell, an overload of the senses, the espresso buzzing beneath my fingertips, even the salt air crinkling my hair.

My sister-in-law, who had bought the camera to take photos of surgical procedures, had generously lent it to me for the trip. I felt and still feel more comfortable recording my impressions with simpler tools: notebook and pen. Opening a camera case, taking off the lens cap, adjusting the many dials of the expensive-looking piece of equipment I borrowed emphasized a primary identity as a tourist I longed to shed. I wanted to be invisible, to fit in, to blend.

I lifted my camera to ask if I could take a picture of their little girl.

"Yes, yes," Sokhi said. Then he conferred with his wife, who turned to their car and fished out a thermos. "You like milk?"

I guessed that they were probably going to offer me some Indian tea (chai: a word that needs no italicization now that it has entered the vernacular, due entirely and somewhat disturbingly to Starbucks.) "Umm, yes. Thank you," I said.

I was surprised then to see his wife pouring what looked like slightly yellowish milk from the thermos into a plastic cup for me. She held out the cup and smiled. I felt obliged to try it, even though I've hated warm milk since I was a child unless it's flavored with chocolate or Ovaltine.

The couple looked at me and smiled. I smiled back. I had gotten myself into this mess.

I took a small sip. Couldn't tell anything. I took another and swallowed gingerly. It tasted like milk sweetened with cardamom and a little sprinkling of saffron, not unlike the drink my mother fixes as prasaad for her morning prayers. It was good. I smiled again, relieved to find out that I could be both polite and enjoy a hot drink. The couple smiled back and held out some biscuits to go with the drink.

Sokhi and I continued to speak in English. He told me he had lived and worked in Dubai for several years. I remembered reading about Indians living and working in the Middle East. The forces of history and immigration leave no place untouched, reflected James Baldwin, writing from a remote Swiss village in the 1950s. "The world is white no longer and will never be white again" ("Stranger in the Village"). This reality only rings truer today, challenging older ideas about borders, nationalities, and identities, and affecting every country.

Sokhi was one of several immigrants, migrants, and sex workers of color I noticed in the cities and small towns of both Sicily and the mainland. During the late 1990s, Italy began to welcome or at least accept more immigrants and other noncitizens. Two reasons for this turn in attitude were the changing internal demographics and the decline in birth rate that had begun after World War II. After decades as a source of economic migrants, Italy's identity shifted to that of a nation that migrants sought to enter or pass through. More recently, in response to the migrant crisis and thousands fleeing war and poverty in the Middle East and North Africa, Italy's populist government has begun refusing to accept refugees.

However, the confluence of cultures on the island is not a new phenomenon. The story of Sicily includes a long history of conquerors and the inevitable cross-pollination of races and ethnicities that such a history produces. The island has always attracted immigrants. Sicilians' complexions, darker than their northern counterparts, reflect the island's ancestry, a crossroads where, among others, the Greeks, the Moors, the Normans, and the Romans settled, and erected monuments, only then to be unseated by the next wave of travelers and fortune seekers. And South Asians? Of course, South Asians live in Italy. I have been known to retort to those who remark on how unusual it is that my mother grew up in Africa that we are everywhere, you can find us everywhere.

I asked if I could take a photo of Sokhi and his family all together. They seemed happy to oblige. We attempted to coax a smile from their little girl. Sokhi asked if I would send him a copy, and I promised I would. He wrote down his name and address. Before I left, Sokhi searched through the jewelry in front of him and lifted up a silver bracelet. "For you," he said. "No, no," I said, "I can't. Let me pay for it." I moved as if to take out my money, but I knew that he wouldn't accept it. I slipped on the bracelet. Their generosity touched me; they did not even know me.

It seemed as if a long time had passed. Fortified by the hot, sweet milk, I felt ready to keep walking and find my classmates. A fish market and fishing boats radiated their pungent smell from one direction, music drifted from a small outdoor carnival area from the other. The shouts of children playing rose above the din of the market. I walked toward the carnival.

I'll admit I had some cynical thoughts. Had they hoped to develop a contact with a U.S. citizen? Had they desired an American present in return? Did they want to ensure a copy of the photo I snapped of their family? These didn't seem like unreasonable things to want. The present of the bracelet seemed like a very Indian gesture to me: to press a gift upon a stranger. Was it because I had looked lost? Or because we had shared a conversation through many fragments of language? Or because we recognized a common past, a history?

♦

After suffering through twelve rolls of photos and my pronouncement that I would keep my clutch of shiny receipts as a reminder of that happy week, my mother shook her head and said, "You must have some previous connection to Italy." Someone would have to ask more than "Where are you from?" to learn about my interest in Sicily.

Is it OK to ask where someone is from? I think that most of us do ask it, in some way. Acquaintances remark that I ask people where they have gone to school; as someone who spent nearly twenty-five years in school, I recognize that it's a way that I classify people—by what they study, by where they study, by how much they've studied. Although intellectually I realize that it's a limited way of understanding where someone is from, it's shorthand I often find myself falling into. It's a classification I despise as well; one of my parents won a scholarship to medical school; the other did not attend college. These facts are unable to convey what I find most admirable and striking about each of them.

How one is asked the question or how one asks it matters. We answer where we come from silently in how we speak, how we dress, where we purchase, if we are able to purchase, how we act, what music we listen to, what books we read. Perhaps it's not entirely possible to answer the question of where we come from, nor is it necessary. I have come to realize that I answer it differently, as do others, depending on to whom I'm telling the story. Still, as a writer and generally curious person, I find myself wanting to know the answer to this question. After having been asked the question so many times, I sometimes think I've earned the right to ask it. That it is a different question for a person of color to ask. And perhaps I fool myself.

When I was younger, walking with my parents in a park or the mall, they would often comment out loud to each other if they saw someone who looked Indian. "Do you think he's Indian?" they would ask each other. And usually, the two families, the other family and my family, would exchange a nod, and a look of recognition might pass between us. It is an old look. We might even stop to talk and say hello. The mall then became a street corner, the roads branching out from cities in the other country. Often, they would ask in Hindi or Gujarati or English, "Where are you from?" Meaning where over *there*. I used to be slightly annoyed by these exchanges. I was clearly from over *here*, in my knock-off Forenza sweater and my short hair; in the way I let my parents answer, and looked around, balancing on the outside edges of my sneakers. These days, I find myself longing for these exchanges, even waiting to see whether or not there will be such a moment, even initiating them.

I didn't realize I would feel drawn to other Indians in Italy, nor that we might mutually wonder about each other's stories of emigration or immigration, and any link we might have beyond a shared sense of having left some place. I remember these exchanges from time to time with the brief sharpness of guilt. After returning to Massachusetts, I got caught up with papers to grade, papers to write. I never organized the pictures and receipts and ticket stubs into a scrapbook or album. I never sent those photos.

[2000, 2019]

Married

We were in the airport. You were sweating so much you needed to find paper towels. You found the usual symbol indicating the usual room. I waited for you, by your bags, watched the people on the rolling walk, standing or walking. Here was all of it: the travel and tiredness. The rolling black suitcases and the pale green suits. The families, the women shuffling in saris, in socks-and-chappals, holding the hands of their grandsons. Everyone and everything was there: people who worked there, the racks of magazines, the packages of dried fruit. I counseled myself not to buy a magazine that I could finish off before the flight. I bought two instead. I wondered where the bride was, and the groom. We had finished a wedding. Were they also in an airport or in a plane? We saw the band from the wedding, waiting for the same flight. They waved us over. "You danced," they said. "A lot," they said. "Have some coffee," they said. "Yes," I said. "I do like to dance." (I wondered then: had I danced too much?)

We were in the small airport. A one-terminal, the kind where it was impossible to miss anyone. We were waiting to get to Detroit, to take the connections back to DC, New York, and the rest. We took the vouchers when the flight was overbooked, and thought about where we could go next. None of us was in a hurry to get back.

We ate some breakfast, the bass player and the trombone player, the groomsman and I. He was not the groomsman I had been carefully seated next to at the rehearsal dinner, nor the one who escorted me back after the service. I was glad to wait for him, but then I wondered why I was waiting. He had his tiny pills for sleep and for no-sleep, and his wife on the East Coast and the silver-gray laptop; he had the noticeably lengthy conversation with a woman at the wedding. The leaning in, the extra drink. I suppose I shrugged; it seemed easier to walk in the airport next to someone, if we were going in the same direction for a while. I wondered, too, about all the people we don't marry.

I composed a postcard to the one groomsman I had been seated not next to, but close by. I wrote it out in my head, then in a notebook, then on the postcard. He called me after he got the card, and I called him back. That was it. We talked about visiting, but that was it: only talk. I can recognize it for what it is. It doesn't mean that I didn't have a good time at the wedding, or at the dinner afterward, but what I am remembering is how we went swimming in Lake Michigan after, and we weren't quite drunk enough. Someone had brought a cooler of drinks to encourage the usual behaviors. The water was warm, the floor pebbly, but still, I was cold. We kept walking out, but the floor never dropped, the water never got deeper. It was strange that way. We crab-walked out, in order to keep ourselves submerged in the water. We stripped to underwear, or underwear and bras, or nothing at all. Some people sat in the gazebo and watched and talked.

Someone I had known in college picked me up and threw me over his shoulder. When we sat down in the lounge chairs on the porch, he sat on me. I was Raggedy-Ann. He said, "I didn't know you could dance like that." His wife said, "Are you comfortable? You can tell him to get off you." Another person sat on top of him; we were tired and silly. I didn't mind the weight of them, of us splayed out on the porch. I didn't mind him seeing me as he had not seen me before. I thought perhaps he should have gone up to their room when his wife went. I thought about all the unspoken things between people. Not everything needs to be said. She knew he'd go swimming and they would travel back to their city on the East Coast.

I went back to my room afterward. Before that, I allowed you, the one I had been carefully seated next to, to think I had fallen asleep on your shoulder in the gazebo. I was as disingenuous as a child who doesn't want to leave. We walked back to the inn, a blanket wrapped around us, and in my room, I gave you my address. I started the water for a bath. I was startled when you came back: perhaps you were bolder than I had imagined. I thought we were both a bit shy. You had left the address I had written out for you on the bed. You came by to get it. We talked a little longer and then you went back to your room. I waited up for another bridesmaid, who would be coming by with someone else from the wedding party. (I had the room key.) They slept on the floor. The next day, we were all tired at breakfast, and traveling back to all the places we had come from and were resigned to returning to. No one, I thought, had found anyone else. Only the couple we had gathered to toast, to surround, to join. I hadn't been thinking of them at all, on their way to sun.

The best line I heard that night: a friend of the groom I had met once before came up to me after several gin and tonics. "Here," he said, "is a string tied around my finger. I tied this string around my finger," he said, "because I wanted to remember to hit on you." I laughed; we danced. The usual songs, in the usual order. He was so ebullient that I wondered. He was kind, and I said, "I have to dance with this other one, the one they've seated me next to. But I will dance this dance with you."

Here is the truth: I wasn't seated directly next to him (too obvious). To you. I mean you. You were at my table, though. What I remember: how you mentioned the punk bands you liked. How you didn't think of yourself as Indian much, but then, you had grown up in New Jersey. Everyone I knew from there thought of other things: I had a cousin who had been into Wicca, another who was briefly interested in NASA, one who dated a Puerto Rican girl, several others who went to NYU.

We had known each other in college, but then, the fact of our Indianness must have been awkward. I liked that you played the guitar. We each did what we did then: went out with other people. You had a Gujarati girlfriend, though, and I couldn't decide if that would make you more likely to want to go out with me, or less. I know one thing should not have to do with the other, but I have always thought of the way each relationship revises the one before. You were finishing one residency and thinking about doing another. I think you had stopped playing in a band, but that you still played sometimes, at home.

I thought about all this, and then we had our few conversations. I called you the way I called everyone I knew in New York that September. Perhaps it would have been smarter to invite you to come visit. An entire weekend of eating out, unfolding the futon, a weekend away from New York. Would I take out my Indian decorations or hide them? Nothing ever came of it. You lived far away from the towers, and you were fine. We talked about the media coverage, we talked about the smoke. I think you had been working in the hospital that day and, like so many others, waited for people who never came.

♥

My mother reminds me of the next one. He is the son of family friends. It is only a reception; the wedding already took place in Bombay. She asks what she should mark on the card: braised vegetables and rice pilaf or the Indian vegetarian dinner? I imagine another round of dancing, toasting, seeing who we are seated next to. I can imagine the cards they will give me. How they will stay in my wallet. (I still have three from the last one. Perhaps I have not been focused enough in following up.) How I will imagine or they will imagine, but we have known each other for years. Calculations. We are getting older. Some of the talk at the tables is always about who is next. Who has a boyfriend or a girlfriend; which ones are not Indian.

At the last wedding, over Columbus Day weekend, I saw my best friend from the time that girls have best friends. She mentioned weekend setups and no one who was working out. "I'm working on it," she said. I said, "I can't seem to do it." In December, her family threw a small engagement party. In the photo she emailed me, she and her fiancé are smiling. I watched the image appear, moment by moment; how it filled the screen.

In one of my mother's small purses I borrow for such occasions are collections of email addresses on smudged napkins or the backs of name cards, which directed us where to sit, and spelled out our names in gold, or silver, in careful sans serif black. I find them, occasionally, when I am looking for other things.

[2002]

Betsy, Tacy, Sejal, Tib

In the books I read growing up, there were always words I couldn't quite imagine. I remember, with a specificity that surprises me, the foreignness of certain colors: *kelly green, strawberry blonde.* These were books about girls with doting fathers and best friends named George, books about an adopted boy named Jim and his sister, Honey. A series about two best friends from the same street who made room for a third. No one felt alone past the second chapter. A series about twins, one good and one slightly more interesting. Like every girl, I wanted a twin or a best friend. Like every girl, I wanted both.

Another series: four girls away at camp—it was in truth a boarding school, but I could scarcely imagine such a thing. That's what I mouthed to myself, then: scarcely. I tried these words on in my head, alone in my room, the bedside lamp on, folded under the covers, escaping into the pages of a book. And isn't that what all writers want? Falling into a book, each one a kind of Narnia, and feeling that exquisite edge of aloneness, honed almost to happiness?

Nearly everything that happened in my life when I was twelve took place at home, or at some close distance from home. My mother would say to me, "Will you get the matching blouse from my drawer? It's popti-colored. Parrot green." In my head, this was the same color as kelly green, but I never found out. I never knew for sure. There were certain colors that bloomed normal on the palette of Indian saris, hanging in rows in the guest bedroom / youngest daughter's closet. The way I'd seen in all of my friends' houses, too—the saris couldn't fit into the parents' closets. Saris and American clothes would not coexist in the same shallow closet of these first homes.

How these series come back to haunt me now, with their sense of ownership over the world, with the ways in which they defined a world. *Kelly green.* With all the ways in which they owned words. *Strawberry blonde.* We read these books, but there was no one like us in any of them. Did we think of writing our own? I want to see us. To see the girl I was, the girls we were, back when we lived at home.

Something like Nancy Drew: *The Secret of the Old Clock, The Clue of the Leaning Chimney. The Mystery of the Girl Who Lives at Home.*

Sejal Shah lived alone with her parents on Pelham Road in western New York State, in a city that had seen better days ("Young Lion of the West"), that had housed stops on the Underground Railroad. She became a late only child, her older brother having jumped ship for college, Brown University, where many of the students were of color, mixed race, radical, or in some other way Third World, yet wanting to begin their training to be doctors, investment bankers, nonprofit organizers, painters, members of the educated elite.

Sejal, when not solving mysteries ("The Case of the Unfinished Homework") or staying away from those less fortunate and more maligned than herself (resource room kids, kids born in India who now faced the horrors of gym class and enforced classroom pairing), spent her days in the company of Esprit-wearing white kids (Jessica, Tara, Amity, Kathleen), trying to avoid the ball in volleyball, running fast in track.

They were incredulous over the obvious: three others in town shared her first name, two shared both her names. It was necessary to use middle initials so as not to confuse the library system and the eye doctor's office: Sejal A., Sejal B., Sejal N. Shah (there was no C.). On the weekend, Sejal A. was joined by her trio of friends. They were all girls with glasses: Sonal, Mini, and Rupali. As you might expect, there were also two boys: Nitin and Manish. Nicky and Max. Even their parents called them by these names, the nicknames an improvement for their junior high lives. Their secret Indian lives—this is what bound them, the Secret Six, together.

During the week, they tried to look like everyone else. On the weekends, they stopped trying. On the weekends, they headed to each other's houses. The girls took turns hosting sleepovers, figuring out which boy they liked. All of them parodied their parents' accents; then they repeated the joke about how their parents ordered a cheeseburger without the burger at McDonald's and asked to talk to the manager, Ronald McDonald, when they were not understood; then they taught each other how to use curling irons to fix their bangs without making awkward cowlick angles.

In each other's kitchens, they ate Hot Mix (Rice Krispies, potato sticks, peanuts, lemon juice, and murchu); practiced moonwalking; kept secret track of who got her period first, watched their mothers making chaa and finding the crushed red pepper to sprinkle on pizza, and their fathers debating something or playing carom. In each other's bedrooms and bathrooms, the girls experimented with hair-removal systems—that noxious cream, Nair, which only sometimes worked, and hydrogen peroxide (sure, some Indians have blonde hair, Sejal tried to tell her brother). In each other's bedrooms, Sejal and Mini gingerly tried out Sally Hansen Natural Cold Wax Kit for Face/Leg/Body/Bikini. Sonal and Sejal tried hot wax with cloth strips and gave themselves minor burns across their legs. Their sensible mothers had warned them about how using a razor would only mean the hair would grow back thicker. Finally, the girls gave up and found the plastic bag of Bic disposable razors one of their fathers used. Then it was time to find Band-Aids and introduce the real topic of conversation: tampons—just how exactly did that work?

In each other's houses, they could relax. No explanations were necessary about why their mothers did or did not wear saris, about what that dot meant (how were they supposed to know?), about the difference between Hindu and Hindi, about why their parents were stricter than American parents, about why they always took their shoes off in the house. They were four girls and two boys. They could have fit neatly into a book.

Boy #1 was the nice one. Boy #2 played the drums. Girl #1 went to school west of the city. She was the only Indian in her school, no small cross to bear in the early '80s. Sonal's mother, Nalini Auntie, was best friends with Sejal's mother, Shobhana Auntie. Girl #2 went to Catholic school—a whole different world from the other girls' schools. Mini wore a uniform, and her school had dress-down days. She and her sister were also the only Indians there. Girl #3 lent Sejal her dress for the eighth-grade formal ("A Night in Paris"). It was a silky gray dress with puffed sleeves. Without Rupali's help, Sejal might have been forced to wear a dress her mother liked. Sejal's mother often said, "School is not a fashion parade!" and Sejal, Sonal, Rupali, and Mini would laugh, because all of their parents said it. And, of course, school *was* a fashion parade. The girls had to know what to wear. This mattered even more if you looked different.

Rupali's father, Sumant Uncle, always drove the kids to the multiplex. The girls watched their little sisters and stayed at the movies for hours, slipping from one theater to another, thrilling at seeing even the last fifteen minutes of a movie they didn't like, just to stay a little longer.

Three of the four girls had at least one parent who had grown up in Africa. Sejal wondered if her own parents and her friends' parents somehow felt more comfortable with each other than with other Indians. They, like the girls, had grown up outside of India. They had to approximate India, too. They were playacting, too: outdated gestures, films, food. Some of them must have read the Famous Five books by Enid Blyton, a British series, but all of the kids in that series were white. Sejal and her brother read comic books, Archie, Veronica, and Betty right next to stacks of Amar Chitra Katha books. Arjuna's dilemma over whether or not to fight his cousins on the battlefield held their interest as much as Archie's never-ending struggle between Betty and Veronica. It was a tough choice: Betty was blonde, but Veronica was rich.

I remember us, think back to us, to the dilemmas of any middle-school girl: the mysteries of the notes we wrote each other. Four girls, and someone was always the odd one out. Of the strategies we deployed to catch the boys' attention: HCP = hard, cold, polite. Alternating with F+F: friendly and flirtatious. Those were the only strategies we had. We also tried to learn how to throw a football, how to hit a baseball, how to play pool, how to swim. Who had the words to talk about that other mystery: how to be American, how not to be American?

I wonder if the other girls felt the way I did. That we needed a series portraying fathers who said no dating till college (or ever), with characters eating pani puri and prasaad, emptying out dresser drawers for the cousin who had come to stay for three months or two years. Did they also wonder when peacock blue, henna red, and popti green would appear in those books? When the names Shalini, Neelu, Ajay, and Sunil would appear? There would be no need to describe the color of the characters' hair: all of them would have black hair, maybe with brown highlights as they got older.

And maybe I would have to remember to mention the green and blue and hazel contact lenses the girls began to wear as they got older. I see them still, see all of us still, wearing our glasses. How awkward and beautiful we were, in our fake Izods, in our Sears. How mysterious and cruel we were, how kind and belly-laughable.

I wanted them all: pulp paperbacks, spines broken, or hardbacks in plastic jackets, the slip of paper on the inside page with all of the library stamps, date after date after date. The covers of the older series were painted the brown and red of the late '70s. Muted colors—olive, that weathered Margaret Thatcher blue-gray, lilac-heather on the hardbacks of *Anne of Green Gables*. It is how I think of those summer evenings, those Sunday afternoons. The days Sonal and I used brown paper grocery bags to bring back a stack of books from either of our town libraries. How we stretched out in her room on Avocado Lane, reading, before roller-skating down the driveway, before it was time to set the table for dinner.

The Gujarati Girls Go to (Hindu Heritage Summer) Camp, The Gujarati Girls Go Skiing, The Mystery of the Prasaad

Plate (A Gujarati Girls Mystery), *The Gujarati Girls Go to Panorama Plaza* (to see the latest Molly Ringwald movie—Gujarati Girls Mystery #13), *The Gujarati Girls Get Malaria* (also titled *The Gujarati Girls Go to India*).

My friends now laugh (it seems almost like a novel) at the stories about how I grew up, how we grew up. We took cup baths, never used the dishwasher except as a drying rack, saved tin foil, almost never ate out. Is that world gone? We were more Indian once, I know this. We were something else once. I feel this as a nearly physical ache, this knowledge, because it means I am something else now.

Still, I am telling you this story, I am telling myself this story as a way to remember how we laughed, how we read, how we knew our friendships were different. How we knew our lives were more interesting than Nancy Drew's. I don't know if I was the only one who wanted to see our faces in what we read, to see our split-level houses, our Corningware dishes and Duralex glasses, our fake wood coffee tables with their stacks of *Time* and *Reader's Digest* (not a *New Yorker* anywhere)—our particular blend of suburban Rochester and middle-class Gujarati—but I am the one who became a writer. I am writing this, on a Wednesday afternoon in Western Massachusetts, thinking ahead to when I will see them, my Gujarati girls, next. Wondering if those books, were I to see them now—if they would mean the same thing to me. Betsy, Tacy, and Tib. Trixie Belden. The Girls of Canby Hall. Anne of Green Gables. Nancy Drew. Sweet Valley High. How could they?

♥

Sejal Shah, Manisha Patel, Sonal Dubey, and Rupali Grady were headed to another wedding. "Don't worry," Sejal said, confidently. "I see the way over here to the left." And she led the way to the door, and she opened it.

[2004]

The World Is Full of Paper. Write to Me.

Shahid was the first and only person to call me a Yankee. I met the poet and professor Agha Shahid Ali in 1996 in the Lower Common Room of Adams House, at Harvard University. It was a winter evening in late March, and I braved the cold to attend his reading, part of the series organized by the famed Grolier Poetry Book Shop.

In my memory, Shahid wears a Nehru jacket, something pale in color, and he glows, the way snow glows on certain winter nights. He must have been reading poems from his forthcoming collection, *The Country without a Post Office*, which held the political violence in Kashmir as its backdrop. I can hear him reciting one of my favorite poems, "Farewell": "The paddle is a heart; it breaks the porcelain waves . . . / My memory keeps getting in the way of your history," and the repetition of those evocative words, history and memory.

Shahid brought the audience to laughter throughout the reading, with his quips and witty asides, before and after reciting his beautiful, haunting poems. When I spoke to him afterward, he was kind and encouraging. I told Shahid I had just applied to the MFA program at UMass Amherst, where he was director, and that I hoped to study with him. "Come, come," he said.

Shahid had previously taught at Hamilton College in central New York State. Hamilton is a couple of hours from where I grew up. Shahid once told me that when he landed in that remote part of New York State, he called on everyone—poets and professors—who lived within a couple of hours, to say he had arrived.

Shahid was warm, charismatic, and irreverent. I fell for him the way you fall for someone across the room at a party and then feel compelled to approach. I had not read his poetry extensively at the time, but as soon as I saw and heard him in Cambridge, I was transfixed. My name was a part of his name; I decided it was destiny.

Knowing almost nothing about Kashmir and its history of occupation and violence by the Indian military, I thought of Shahid as simply an Indian American writer. I hoped to find in him a mentor. At the time, I had met only one other South Asian American writer: Bharati Mukherjee, who declared herself an American writer, rejecting any hyphen or descriptor such as Indian American or Bengali American or South Asian American or Asian American. In the mid-1990s, while a student at Wellesley College, I attended one of Mukherjee's readings at Waterstones bookstore in Back Bay, Boston. Other South Asians were in the audience, and we looked at each other with interest and at her with a kind of hunger. We wanted to see writers who looked like us, who wrote about South Asians in the United States, or who embraced a bicultural or multiethnic identity. I was disappointed to learn Mukherjee did not want to be read in that context. However, I can't blame her—I believe in self-definition. She wished to be understood and accepted as an American writer—as American as anyone else.

The literary landscape was different then. This was before Jhumpa Lahiri won the Pulitzer in 2000. It was before

Salman Rushdie curated the special Indian fiction section of the June 23 and 30, 1997, issue of the *New Yorker*, which marked India's fiftieth anniversary of independence from British rule; the issue (with a statue of Ganesh in what looks like a jungle and two white explorers with Indiana Jones–type hats looking at him on the cover—the reader meant to identify with that white gaze) heralded South Asian writers' arrival to American literary audiences by the powers that be. This was before UMass Amherst MFA program's own Kamila Shamsie (Shahid's protégé and student at both Hamilton College, where he previously taught, and UMass) published the first of several novels, and before Kiran Desai won the Man Booker Prize in 2006.

When I arrived in Amherst in the fall of 1997 to study fiction, I asked Shahid right away if I could take his poetry workshop. It was more unusual then for poets and fiction writers to take workshops in a genre other than their own (it is a requirement now), but Shahid ignored the genre tribes and welcomed me into his class. "Sure," he said. "Why not?"

In addition to MFA students, our workshop included a local high school teacher, as well as the poet Kevin Goodan, who commuted to Amherst from New York City once a week; Shahid, ever inclusive, turned no one away. In class critiques, around a long, rectangular table, Shahid often rewrote our poems, starting from the bottom, working his way to the top. He suggested new possibilities for each of us, reading his revisions in a lilting voice. This rewriting occasionally hurt my feelings, often bewildered me, and sometimes infuriated me. I remember the extensive reordering of my poem "Alexander Street" in Shahid's distinctive handwriting in fountain pen ink. In that poem, the first line became, instead, the twenty-eighth. Shahid crossed out so many lines in another poem, "Palette," that out of the original twenty-five lines of the poem, only eight remained. In "The Simple Dark," which I had revised once, he reordered the stanzas to 2-4-3-6-1-5, taking a concluding verse in the poem, moving it up to the middle, and shuffling the rest.

I was horrified. In college my poems had received every undergraduate literary prize awarded. No one had taken my writing apart, line by line, and so swiftly dismantled their basic architecture, what I thought of as the poem's intention and integrity. Still, despite my discomfort, I could see that Shahid was doing something interesting. I must have understood I needed to pay attention, because even after sixteen years I have held on to all of Shahid's written comments on my work.

One month into the semester, Shahid delivered a piece of advice to me, announced to our entire workshop: "Never use the word *soul* in a poem!" he declared and then grinned. He was both teasing and completely serious. I winced. I had just brought in a villanelle, "Onyx, Obsidian, Phlox, Coal," in which *soul* was one of the repeating end words. I have remembered his dictum through the years and have heard myself saying it to my own students: we want our poems and stories to be *soulful*—to possess qualities of the infinite in them—but it is difficult for the word *soul* to do the work of that desire, particularly in undergraduate writing. A word such as *soul* often functions too abstractly—it lacks the concrete detail and specific imagery to make a vital and elusive idea visible and material.

Though regularly miffed by his handling of my poems (*Where was the unadulterated praise?*), I was, like everyone,

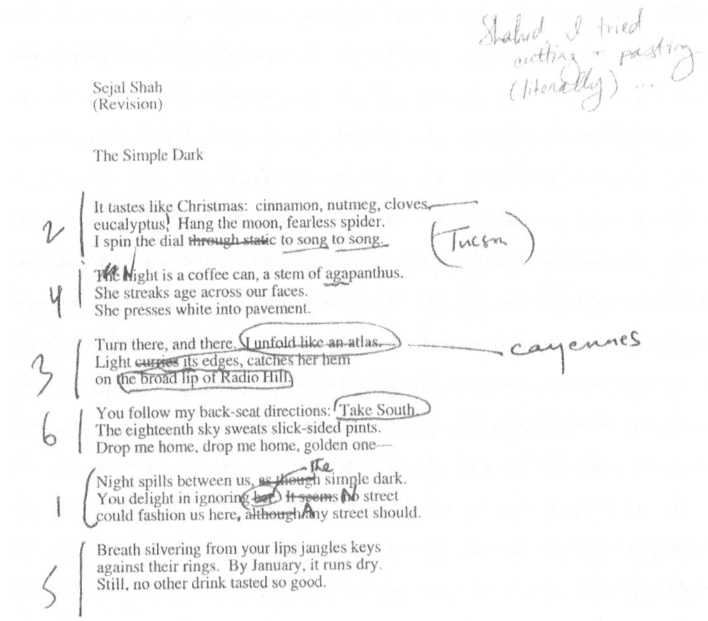

The Simple Dark

It tastes like Christmas: cinnamon, nutmeg, cloves,
eucalyptus. Hang the moon, fearless spider.
I spin the dial through static to song to song.

The Night is a coffee can, a stem of agapanthus.
She streaks age across our faces.
She presses white into pavement.

Turn there, and there. I unfold like an atlas.
Light curries its edges, catches her hem
on the broad lip of Radio Hill.

You follow my back-seat directions: Take South.
The eighteenth sky sweats slick-sided pints.
Drop me home, drop me home, golden one—

Night spills between us, as though simple dark.
You delight in ignoring bay. It seems no street
could fashion us here, although any street should.

Breath silvering from your lips jangles keys
against their rings. By January, it runs dry.
Still, no other drink tasted so good.

(Handwritten annotations: "Shahid, I tried cutting + pasting (literally) ..."; numbers "2", "4", "3", "6", "1", "5" beside stanzas; "Tucson"; "cayennes"; "the")

"The Simple Dark," a poem I submitted to Agha Shahid Ali's poetry
workshop, fall 1997, Amherst, Massachusetts. Even my revision got
revised and reordered!

still taken by Shahid—admiring both his exquisite poetry
and his generous nature.

In our workshop, Shahid would recite each one of our
names as though it were a poem, brilliant, somehow mi-
raculous and mysterious, complete and gorgeous in and of
itself. "Daniel!" he'd say, delightedly. "Daaa-niel Haaaales."
(He loved Daniel Hales's name, but in truth it seemed as if
he loved all of our names.) "It's the wonderful Kelly Le Fave!
James Heflin. Carrie St. George Comer. Andrew Vaaar-non.
Robert N. Casper!"

Shahid believed in gathering everyone together; he believed in joy—he embodied it. After our workshop sessions, he often suggested we continue the conversation over drinks in town at the Amherst Brewing Company. *This*, I thought, *is graduate school*. I didn't realize then that this was just Shahid.

Twice that fall he invited our class as well as other students and friends for hours-long, sprawling dinner parties. People spilled over from room to room—Shahid had many friends and admirers, and we all basked in his warmth. When I offered to help cook for one of his parties, Shahid laughed and said, "You American-born Indians are the most terrible cooks." I couldn't argue. I was taken aback, but had to laugh.

One evening, when the stove burners were not working and the food had to be warmed up elsewhere, Shahid charmed us for hours as only an exceptionally good host could, playing Hindi film music and ABBA. (*Why not? The perfect Shahidian combination!*) No one minded not eating for a while—we may well not have even noticed. I remember he broke into song. "Hey," I said, "I know that song," and began dancing in his Northampton home, performing the Bharata Natyam dance steps I had learned as a child. Shahid clapped his hands in encouragement. "Vah, vah!" he said. Finally—the subcontinental applause I had been waiting for!

His expansive nature was a striking contrast to the awkward self-consciousness so often true of writers. In *Best American Poetry 1997*, above his poem "Return to Harmony 3," he wrote, "To my subcontinental darling across the continents—love—of course."

In my copy of *The Country without a Post Office*, he filled the entire front page with his effusive script in blue fountain pen ink (now slightly faded):

for SEJAL—
—Shah of Shahs!—
—so royal, so princely—
so regal—so she
who couldn't go to Spain
is going to Italy!
———— Ah!————

He decorated this note with long dashes flourishing on either side of the "Ah!," almost spanning the width of the page.

Warmly, Kisses—
Shahid
19 Feb '98
Amherst

Later, he continued in another pen:

& now——where is lipstick?
Purple?——Of colour?——
Sejal has the magic!

Who else could have written about the purple lipstick I wore that year at his book signing, when all of us had crammed into Wootton's, a narrow bookstore in downtown Amherst, for the *Best American Poetry* reading—in a way that transformed my name, travel plans, and shade of lipstick into near poetry? It was what we all wanted—what anyone wants from someone he or she admires—and certainly what I wanted—for him to see the magic that is only you.

I cannot imagine my time in the MFA program without Shahid—without those warming dinner parties in wintry Massachusetts, without remembering our poems unwritten, in order for different possibilities to be imagined.

As a professor and teacher myself for over a decade now, I understand his rewriting, painful as it was for me, as another form of attention, even as another kind of love. It is a strategy I use too—unwriting, rewriting, undoing—in the workshops I now teach. I think of Shahid when I attempt to respond to students' poems honestly, generously, usefully. It's much easier to shy away from the declaration that a poem is not quite working and to instead merely praise what is easily praiseworthy, but what has stayed with me all these years is the more honest, if often ego-bruising, critique. I can see now that Shahid was trying to lessen my dependence on strict narrative, my desire to tell a story within a poem, and to instead allow the poem to unfold, to breathe, to surprise, to live, through the generation of lyric possibilities.

During my first year of graduate school, Shahid was the director of the MFA program, and I had reason to call him once or twice at home. His answering machine message was simply, "I knew you'd call," emphasis on the *knew*. No preamble. The first time I heard it, I hung up. As usual, Shahid had caught me off guard. His outgoing message sounded like a line from one of his poems, a moment of delight, of enchantment. His voice left me speechless and smiling.

Shahid's message was to the point and too short—like his life. No time to think of what to say, to fill the space with unnecessary words. We flocked to him: students, poets, and writers—ambitious dreamers. I see him in his Northampton kitchen, turning toward me in a royal blue sweater, his shirt sleeves unbuttoned and pushed back: he is cooking for us. I've snapped a photo and caught him off guard in the picture—but he's still posing, still gesturing—still lovely, still young. He would hate me saying so, but his eyes look soulful. *I knew you'd call.*

[2013]

Postscript

There was little room for my voice in Shahid's workshop, and the cutting away of my words did hurt. I was not entirely honest when I said it didn't. I don't teach that way now. I appreciate what Shahid did and who he was and loved him for it, but I also learned that was not the way I wanted to help my students find their voices. I will never cook like Shahid, and I will never teach like him. I miss him, and I am grateful to have found my way back to writing, writing letters to my younger self, to people I have loved and lost, to people who left and people who wounded; the impulse to write is mine. The world is full of paper. I am writing now. I am writing to me. I am writing to myself and others like me.

[2018]

Kinship, Cousins, & Khichidi

Several years ago, when my Italian boyfriend returned to Italy and to a girlfriend he had told me was an ex, I stopped eating. Even a steady diet of soap operas as a child had not spared me from a clichéd story line. I suffered in all of the usual ways. Why eat? I could spoon ramen noodle soup from cardboard and Styrofoam cup containers in which food = add hot water—if I had remembered to buy the containers. The prospect of going to the store overwhelmed me: all those lights, all those choices, brands, people. I lived on what was in my fridge and cabinets: orange juice, coffee, the occasional package of ramen. I have always been thin, but that fall I dropped to under a hundred pounds. I am 5'6". In not a particularly graceful way, I fell apart.

I spent much of that year in Amherst on my uncomfortable couch (older brother's old futon), watching an embarrassing number of *Party of Five* and *Beverly Hills 90210* reruns and uniformly uplifting stories on the Lifetime "Television for Women" series *Intimate Portrait*. I sat through multiple episodes of *Behind the Music*—anyone else's fall from grace, subsequent despair, and triumphant recovery cheered me. My friends rallied and took turns showing up at my door with takeout or dragging me out of my apartment to brunch.

"We'll be over in half an hour," they'd announce to my answering machine. "We know you're there." Eating together, laughing and talking, helped me realize that although I did miss the Italian, much of what I missed was companionship. Eventually I took up the cause; he wasn't going to call or come back, and I had a life to live. (You know: *One Life to Live*—even if I'm Hindu and supposedly have more.) I downed cans of coffee-flavored Ensure between meals, finally admitting that it was too tiring and costly to choose not to eat. If I didn't eat—couldn't eat—I was not going to finish graduate school or write a book or even be able to finish a thought, let alone be able to repay the favor and cook for my friends.

I fell for the Italian partly because he cooked. He often called to see if I wanted to come over for dinner on his nights to cook for his host family. I lived around the corner from them in Amherst, maybe four houses away. The meal I remember most: Chinese eggplants the color of a bruise, gleaming as if they had been waxed and buffed, sliced into circles the thickness of three silver dollars, sautéed with garlic and garnished with single leaves of basil, beautiful disks shining with olive oil. We polished our plates with slices of his host mother's homemade bread, punctuating food and conversation with swallows of cold, slightly sour white wine. Nothing fancy, but I felt civilized. I was so happy with this food: it brought me back to a recent trip to Italy, the setting of a few of the happiest days of my life.

It seems to me now the most intimate kind of relationship and socializing: cooking and inviting others over to eat—although when I was younger, it just seemed to be about work: more and more work, always for women.

I never wanted to learn how to cook. I saw what it did for my mother and all of the other aunties: who wants to spend their life in the kitchen, wiping oil splatters off the stove range, scouring the kitchen sink with Comet, hands in plastic yellow gloves, filling Corning dishes with leftovers?

Moms in the kitchen, making chaa. It was the 1980s: everyone piled out of station wagons, those Cutlass Cruisers with fake wood paneling. We trooped into the house, shoes off without being told. Moms boiling milk, getting out the glass container with ilaychi for swaad. The rising and falling of voices laughing-talking in Gujarati, different to my ears from English-on-the-phone, English-with-the-neighbors. Moms trying to find the saansee before the milk boils over, getting out the naasto: peanuts and potato sticks and crisps, hot mix. They dispatched one or two of us to the backyard, out by where the scraggly grass grew at the far side of the yard, to pluck a few mint leaves for chaa. The men slouched on the sofa and easy chairs, talking about whatever men talk about. (Sports? Kids? Jobs at Xerox/Kodak? I never listened closely.)

I went to the Kids' Room: the basement or the family room, or wherever the other kids had stashed themselves or had been stashed. We sat on the floor for dinner, happily staining our hands with cholé and batakaa ni shaak with rotli, sometimes throwing sweets at each other, prasaad on those Gita Sundays—laadvaa, pendaa, barfi. Then the girls are called into the kitchen for kitchen duty. The boys escaped to the TV: to the game (whatever game was on, it was understood that they had to watch it) or to the basement to play table tennis or pool or kickball, only occasionally saddled with watching the youngest of us. Who wouldn't want to be a boy then?

The women fought good-naturedly over who would wash the dishes, load the dishwasher, clear the table, and so on. I wanted to be in the living room, patting my stomach, chomping away on dhaaran dhaar and valyaarie, after-dinner digestives and breath fresheners—the container passed companionably from person to person.

In a story I wrote about the Italian/Ensure/*Party of Five* period of my life, I recall a line: "Who will want to marry an Indian girl who hates to cook?" I didn't want to be anyone's passage to India. I didn't want to get married right away. I didn't want to be the woman in the kitchen, still making rotlis when the rest of the family is sitting down so that the rotlis are hot: first one to the father (husband), then to the son (brother), then to the daughter. I think the daughter was supposed to be up and helping. I wanted to sit down, legs stretched. I'm ashamed to admit it (my hardworking mother), but I wanted to slouch.

3. BROOKLYN & AMHERST

I joined the Park Slope Food Co-op because I wanted to be able to walk out the door of my yoga studio (next door to the co-op) and satisfy my craving for an overpriced Fresh Samantha smoothie and a bar of Chocolove: dark chocolate with orange peel. I peered in at the women with good haircuts—their European clogs and hand-knit wool sweaters—at the mothers with babies who were different colors than themselves, at the many dreadlocked heads. The fresh-faced woman behind the desk ate tofu and noodles from a plastic container. The woman next to her worked on her needlepoint, chatted easily about kids and the neighborhood, and checked people in. You have to be a member to shop, they told me. The co-op reminded me of Amherst, and although I had moved partly to live somewhere different and more diverse, I suppose we are drawn to what is familiar. I went to a membership meeting. Despite my irritation at the complicated work shifts and rules, I was secretly pleased at belonging to something in the middle of the largest city in which I'd ever lived.

My last year living in Western Massachusetts, I belonged to a CSA (community supported agriculture) farm, splitting a share with friends who taught at Mount Holyoke. My vegan friend Michael, who composts religiously and grows some of his own food outside of the Adirondack State Park, remarked, "Everyone who joins a CSA says that it changes their relationship with food." It did for me, as well. Some weeks I harvested more vegetables than I could possibly cook and knocked on neighbors' doors to offer an extra ear of corn or an acorn squash. I liked meeting more of my neighbors. I tried to figure out how to cook a long thin squash I had seen but never bought (glancing over them in the produce section of Stop & Shop), sautéed Swiss chard and collard greens, learned how to boil and mash turnips to prepare a side dish, something not unlike mashed potatoes.

I wandered through the beds of peonies, sunflowers, fuchsia cosmos, and brown-eyed Susans at the farm, greedily filling my arms, eating nearly all of the raspberries I gathered. I picked many different kinds of tomatoes and basil for a salad my friend Elliot had showed me how to make years ago, when those kinds of salads and fresh mozzarella cheese were exotic to me. They signified to me the Italophile culture of academia and art that I wanted to be able to navigate. It was an American salad, something I would not have learned how to make at home. These were new words and adjectives: *extra virgin olive oil, balsamic vinegar, capers*—acquired after college, rolling carefully off my tongue, filed away under *intellectual, upper middle class, American*.

One summer at the local farmer's market I remember stopping to talk to a young woman, her hair pushed back from her face with a blue cotton kerchief. She sat behind a table, slices of tomatoes in front of her, some purple, some yellow, some the standard red I recognized from the store. Heirloom tomatoes, she explained. Some of the tomatoes tasted like summer, sweet and tangy—completely unrelated to the cardboard-tasting, plump, Christmas-red variety I knew. Still, I thought: *granola*. Who would possibly devote their Saturday mornings to educating the public about purple tomatoes? Only the fringe of food eaters. I could not even imagine such devotion.

4. FLUSHING, JACKSON HEIGHTS, TORONTO, CHINATOWN, NORTHAMPTON

My parents took us to Jackson Heights, Queens, and Gerrard Street in Toronto for Indian groceries years before I ever set foot in India. The India I know lives in North America. I remember longing for an Indian section of the Upstate New York city I grew up in. I wanted a version of the Chinatowns my uncles took me to in San Francisco and Oakland whenever I visited them. It meant we existed. Sari shops and music, bootlegged videos of the latest Hindi film, the soundtrack blaring from outside the storefronts, grandfathers drinking tea and spitting tobacco on the sidewalk in front of their sons' stores. Young girls asleep on a stack of Kashmiri rugs near the cash register, coconut-oiled braids flung to one side.

During the last couple of years I lived in Massachusetts, I found my family of friends through food. We ate together on a regular basis: Vietnamese pho or Jamaican red peas and rice from Springfield, bi bim bop at the Korean place on Route 9, South Indian food in Queens, sambar-idli with coconut and mint chutneys from the Haymarket in Northampton, asparagus and mushrooms marinated in soy sauce and garlic, cooked on the George Foreman grill of good friends, eaten on their screened-in porch. Food became a language, a way of sharing experiences and talking, something more appealing to me than always going out for a drink.

We lounged and lingered at each other's homes; we discussed food in great detail; we wanted seconds even after we were done with ice cream and tea. We extended Saturday night into Sunday and made brunch plans. I thought of the Gujarati Indian community I grew up in, where food was part of the point of getting together. Growing up with parents who don't drink, and who socialized around food, religion, and conversation, I associate alcohol with American life. I associate food with family.

On my last visit to New York City before I moved there, some friends and I drove down to Flushing and then took the train to Jackson Heights. Flushing shocked me, reminding me briefly of the Shanghai I had visited fifteen years earlier. I hadn't known what an Asian–Asian American city it was. On the train between Flushing and Jackson Heights, the seats were filled with people who looked like us—various shades of brown, we marveled silently to each other. We ate our way through Chinese food, then South Indian food, tearing pieces of a paper-thin, buttery dosa filled with potatoes, and then pani puri: finally, Gujarati food. I loved being able to take my friends from Western Massachusetts to my food.

Before driving back to Northampton, we ended up in a Malaysian restaurant, marveling at the mix of East Asian and South Asian food. We wanted to stay and stay, and talked about canceling our Friday appointments, calling in sick to work. I wanted to be able to eat the food of my childhood. I know it's easier to just learn how to make it than to live near Gerrard Street, Jackson Heights, Edison, Waltham, my mother.

On the way back to Route 91, crossing the Whitestone Bridge, we already began to reminisce about dumplings, various pieces of meat I don't want to remember as the only vegetarian in the group, savoring the new sensation of sucking up the tapioca balls in bubble tea, of being satiated, reveling in our stash of Bollywood DVDs and still pressing our fingertips lightly to our eyebrows. All of us had gotten our eyebrows threaded in Jackson Heights, on a break from eating. We had left the country without a passport and returned with expressions of perennial surprise stemming from somewhat severely, somewhat delicately arched eyebrows. We decided against mehndi, but I think we wanted some outside marker of this inside trip, something to match the spread of our stomachs, some physical articulation of the well-being we felt, that lift and expansion in our hearts.

The opportunity to move to New York came up unexpectedly, and I jumped at it. I rented a room in a good friend's Park Slope apartment, about eight blocks, it turned out, from one of my second cousins. I had met Suketu and his wife and sons four years ago in Bombay, where they had lived while he worked on a nonfiction book about the city. The Mehtas are not a branch of the family I knew while growing up—my path crossed with Suketu's parents and sisters only at large family weddings (he was already launched into his own life). My closer relatives kept telling me I should meet him, the other creative writer in the family. I was apprehensive and a little shy about meeting a relative by email and showing up at his apartment in India. I did it anyway. Suketu and his wife graciously hosted me for a couple of days. I still remember meeting them in the morning (they had been out when I arrived the night before). "Hi," they said. "Coffee?" It was awkward meeting, all of us in our pajamas with morning hair, but they put me at ease. Suketu made a spicy corn-and-mushroom dish for dinner that night. I still remember it, his cooking and chatting with me. He teased me about what a slow eater I am. That's something else that my relatives do—tease me.

In Brooklyn, I was sitting at Ozzie's, a coffee shop on Fifth Avenue across from my apartment, trying to write, when Suketu walked by. Having never lived near any of my extended family, it was the only time I'd ever just "run into" one of them. Ozzie's, a cafe with lots of tables for writers to park themselves for hours with their laptops and cappuccinos, boasted one unbroken wall of windows adjacent to the sidewalk. We waved at each other, and Suketu came in to chat. "Come over for dinner soon," he said. "My in-laws arrive this week." Lots of people say come over, and lots of people don't follow up. We all know how it is: life gets in the way. But Suketu did call, and I did walk over for dinner: delicious, spicy South Indian food that his mother-in-law had cooked. This is how I know we're related. I realize, in writing this, that kinship for me involves food.

One rainy afternoon when I was sick, Suketu came by with khichidi, a mix of yellow lentils and rice that my mother always made when we weren't feeling well. I had just been heating up instant tomato soup (another comfort food) when my cousin called. My cough, dramatic, phlegmy, inserted itself like static into our conversation, making it difficult to talk.

"You sound miserable," he said.

"Yeah. What can you do?" I said.

"What kind of food would make you feel better?"

I thought about what my mom would make, food that seems too labor-intensive or thought-intensive when I'm sick. "Khichidi or upama, I guess."

"I'll bring some over later," he said.

"That's sweet of you to offer," I told him, "but you don't have to do that." You can prevail upon your own family, but second cousins are under no obligation to do anything.

"No problem," he said. "I'll just stop by on my way out. I'm meeting friends for dinner."

"Khichidi delivery," Suketu said when he buzzed the door later. He presented me with a plastic bag holding a yogurt container filled with khichidi and a small bottle of spicy garlic pickle—"good for the taste," he said, "and to chase the cold away."

Underscoring family, proximity, a way of expressing caring. Another writer friend from India told me that he doesn't think the term "cousin-sister" exists in American English: you are either a cousin or a sister, a cousin or a brother. But in Indian English (including what I grew up speaking), what you say is cousin-brother, cousin-sister.

Suketu and I are distant enough relatives that our kinship has something to do with choice. We met as adults, share none of the childhood memories I associate with my first cousins. Suketu cooked up some khichidi that I didn't know how to make and brought it over. This is how, in some specific and fundamental way, I recognize that he's Indian, that I know that he's family. I know he would laugh at this, but it is true.

My cousin loves to cook. But someday if he is not feeling well, I would like to be able to bring over some food—though he happens to be married to a good cook himself, and has a sister of his own living nearby. That's not just what an Indian girl would do, it's what a cousin-friend does, what a cousin-sister does. I'm leaving Brooklyn soon to return to the Pioneer Valley, aka Western Massachusetts. I will remember that khichidi and garlic pickle. Will remember that I want to cook for others, to invite them to my house, to my apartment, to feed them. And isn't that what love is: feeding and being fed?

6. MASSACHUSETTS, NEW HAMPSHIRE, GOA, ZANZIBAR, KENYA

After five years in the Land of Mediocre Indian Food, my comfort food of choice is Chinese. I want sautéed greens and straw mushrooms. I want dragon skins: deep-fried tofu skins stuffed with vegetables and long thin sprouts from The Great Wall. It's a restaurant in Florence, Massachusetts, in a strip mall that reminds me of places near where I grew up: sad fluorescent lighting in the parking lot, a nondescript storefront sandwiched between a drug store and a liquor store. It's the best Chinese food in the area, away from the tourist-happy, storybook Main Street of Northampton. The Indian restaurants in the area left me hungry. I was disappointed after half-heartedly spooning lukewarm coconut soup at one, paying one or two dollars for "papadum and condiments" at another (tamarind chutney, mango pickle, onion and tomato—really the equivalent of a basket of chips and salsa at a Mexican restaurant).

My friend Karen had me over for dinner a couple of years ago. "Nothing fancy," she said. "I'll just throw a veggie burger on, and you can hang out with the kids and John." We sat down. The metal Indian spice tin (dubbo) that is usually filled with round steel containers of geeru, thanageera, erther, hing, meetu, murchu instead held an equally colorful mix of American condiments—mayonnaise, ketchup, mustard—and was passed around the table. My mother presented me with a dubbo when I moved into my first apartment: a round stainless-steel container, like a tin filled with Christmas cookies, except with smaller round containers inside with no lids, six around the edges and one in the middle. I could imagine my grandmother presenting a similar tin to my mother when she got married and left to set up her own household—something in the gesture suggested this. If I feel around the edges of the duubo, I find my name engraved in Gujarati.

Like my mother, Karen grew up partially in Kenya. We are Indian through the diaspora, and each permutation, each immigration and variation, fascinates me. She also grew up in New Hampshire, the daughter of Goan Kenyan immigrants who themselves grew up in Zanzibar. Karen has never been to India. I told Karen that her duubo, filled as it was with American "spices," was the perfect image for a book cover. How can we not adapt to the new country? I remember the feeling—visceral, jolting—and the laughter at what is familiar placed in an unfamiliar way: all the standard condiments and the familiar stainless-steel container. Karen, the mother of two young kids, has an admirably practical manner. The visual combination of ketchup and duubo struck me as indelibly and particularly American.

7. NEW YORK, MASSACHUSETTS, THE MIDWEST, THE SOUTH

In the year I've lived in New York, I've never actually made it back to Jackson Heights, although I mean to, it is on my list. Park Slope isn't known for its Indian food: when I don't feel like cooking, I grab a veggie burger with chipotle mayonnaise on the side downstairs at Bonnie's Grill, or a Baja Burrito from La Taqueria on Seventh Avenue.

Throughout my childhood I thought baklava, the Middle Eastern dessert made with pastry dough, chopped nuts, and honey, was Indian food because my mother made it. I remember helping her lay down the filo sheets in layers, using a special food brush, dunking the brush in a bowl of melted butter, drizzling, then painting the sheets until they shone, the color of light. I remember the sound of the brush, not unlike the ghee-filled chumchee across a stack of rotlis, a paper noise—quiet, soothing. The sound of her bangles falling back and forth down her arms.

All the food we were teased about while growing up has become chic now. At parties, people ask me if I know how to make naan, and relay in detail what usually works for them. One of my best friends from graduate school, a white guy, makes the best saag paneer I have ever eaten (sorry, Mom).

Even now, I find it difficult to eat alone—it's not how Indians eat, I think. It's hard to enjoy food without talk. Eating is communal: what is food without sharing, without laughing, without pressing seconds on one other? I have had to learn to eat by myself in order to survive, but eating that way has always felt counterintuitive to me. Every day, the problem of what to make. Why can't I take a pill and be done with it, all of the day's nutrients and fat and carbohydrates and protein and calcium? More time to run around, read, go to book signings and parties. More time for the important things.

I never found such a pill. Instead, I find that if I don't eat, I am simply too tired to walk from work to the parking lot. I have to rethink what the important things are.

So I'll turn the TV on to *Friends* or *Entertainment Tonight*, and go back to the kitchen to cut up potatoes, onions, for cholé. Energy for yoga class, for tomorrow's run. To just be able to teach my class well. Sometimes I'll talk on the phone. The background noise helps. I'm older now: I have to cook. I have to eat.

I'm leaving New York in a few weeks, but I plot my return. Like many of my Asian American friends, I'm hesitant to live in the Midwest or the South, the wrongly perceived homes, I know, of terrible Indian food. I'm returning to Massachusetts. Still, how can I say that I don't want to live in a place with mediocre Indian food? Unless I become a better cook—until I become a better cook—any place I am is suspect.

[2003]

Street Scene

Parisians call this neighborhood mixed. Mixed is code; it means immigrants. "Think Brooklyn," Caitlin says. We are in the Twentieth Arrondissement, near Père Lachaise. I am here to see the Louvre and the Turkish baths; I am here to visit my friend Caitlin. I have a map and some time for wandering. To travel by yourself and enjoy it is a skill; I don't practice it enough.

The Twentieth Arrondissement. Storefronts with fuchsia and blue signs; Senegalese behind tables of patterned scarves, watch caps, and leather bags; music, a low flare around which we warm ourselves at the park, at pool tables, at long wooden bars. LeeAnne isn't here to tell me where she stayed in Paris. When I think of her, I see us talking in my backyard, splashing in the pool, Upstate New York summers. It surprises me. She was never there, but I can see it: the blue pool, our hideaway; beach towels; instant iced tea. I imagine we lay ourselves out on the uneven flagstones, waiting to be hot enough to peel ourselves off and fling ourselves into the water. If I close my eyes hard enough, if I squint, I can almost see it, this scene— that we grew up together. She was that kind of friend. As I walk through Paris, I keep expecting to catch a glimpse of her, vanishing into some narrow street.

Paris is a walking city; even my softest black shoes will produce blisters. We are on the Champs-Élysées, on the way to a makeup store to have our eyes made up. Caitlin and her roommate are going to a birthday party tonight. I am back in seventh grade, conjugating verbs, acting out a skit in which we say, "Where is the party? I'll meet you there. We will see you there. I will see you there. See you there?"

Caitlin and I were neighbors toward the end of our twenties. I am staying with her in Paris for a week. We are neighbor-friends—neighbors who became friends—friends who once lived close by. She moved into our apartment complex, two doors away from me. She wore pencil skirts, perfectly tailored, unusual to see in a graduate student in our hippie college town. I admired her. Then her new boyfriend showed up, playing guitar, sitting out on the back porch, and I felt shy. And I was embarrassed. He was someone I had known from the university years before. We had once, twice had two beers too many and kissed awkwardly in the apartment he shared with two other musicians. The years passed; he and Caitlin broke up. Now neither of us is in touch with him, and I fly across an ocean to visit her.

The word for neighbor is *la voisine*. The word for sister is *ma sœur*. Friends are *les amies*.

Each day, I walk across the street to the internet café. There is something comforting in something you do every day. Repetition, even across one week, is key. This is what I say to the Senegalese man who works there: "*Un café au lait et un pain au chocolat, s'il-vous-plaît.*" He answers in French rather than in the English we both know he knows. I take this as a kindness.

I take the Metro to the Musée d'Orsay. I look at paintings everyone recognizes. I dig my camera out from between pens and street map and take pictures: a long-faced woman; a flock of ballerinas in blue tulle and chiffon; a rooster; a bride and groom, suspended.

We sang songs in seventh grade. *Alouette, gentille alouette.* Skylark, nice skylark, I will pluck the feathers off of you. I will pluck the feathers off your head, off your back; I will break your beak. I will remove your heart. I am going to dismember you. This is what runs through my head: French class. Even though I am in France.

I came to Paris to make up for seven years of French in grade school. What do you do with a language you never use? I didn't know when I booked my flight what I was looking for. I had a friend in France. I thought, *Why not?*

We had a concrete pool in the backyard of my parents' house, but it no longer exists. My parents filled it in five years ago. They hired someone to break down the raised rim; they must have rented a crane to fill the hole with earth. My brother and I saw pictures, but we were not there to see the pool in which we spent our summers lifted away and filled. We were not there to see the yellow bulldozers or the torn wooden fence. We did not see the truck full of earth brought to reclaim the kidney-bean shape: curved, fetal. We saw the earth there, without grass, sinking. More dirt needed to be brought in to cover the indentation of what was gone, what had left.

Once, LeeAnne spent two weeks by herself in Paris at museums. I could barely do two days. We met when I was twenty-four, close to too late for meeting a friend you could love as if you were young. I rushed in, late to an orientation for a new job; she put her hand on the chair next to her. "Here," she said. I sat down, embarrassed, out of breath. She leaned over and whispered, "You didn't miss anything. You're fine!" Her face opened up whenever she saw me, as though I were the most precious and wonderful present in her life—a rare flower, a perfect day. She was like that with all of her friends. She made you feel—by the quality of her attention, her shining hazel eyes, her rapt, joyful smile—loved.

I was looking at a painting. I stood shaking in front of flowers: dull flowers, heads bent. I knew she had been happy. I knew nothing. She is gone. What do we really know about anyone else? Or their sorrow? The flowers were alive and painful to gaze at: brown, fading; green and purple, thick paint, too thick, streaks nearly grotesque, almost lovely, nearly gorgeous. I cried in front of the other tourists. I wanted to find her. She was gone. I closed my eyes. I wanted to see her once more. I want to see her again.

There is no one on the street in this street scene. The scene is the angle at which the road curves and so it seems to open up, to hold some possibility. The paintings are the signs for *l'hôtel* and *pâtisserie*. The color is the color of fall leaves. The only figure is a church steeple, slate gray. I remember walking alone though I was in a city, a much-walked city, and I must never have seen a corner that empty. In Paris, I feel as if I am walking, again and again, across a stage set. The entire city stands still, posed, as if a museum or a photograph.

We could see the cemetery from Caitlin's apartment. Important people were buried there, I'd been told. I pressed myself against Caitlin's window and took pictures of the gravestones. Who was there? Van Gogh, Degas, Giacometti, Modigliani? No. It was Morrison, Stein, Chopin, Proust. LeeAnne would have chosen more time with the art, not bothering with the cemetery. I thought of the flower heads bowing at the museum, irises bending, shrinking back. I thought of the mint tea from the hammam, the sharp-scented blue soap, the hands of women I don't know on my back. I thought of LeeAnne gazing up at the Chagall; she would have been transfixed by the violet sky, clasped arms, bound by the colors, turning to someone in delight. She would have been breathless. Nine years later, one fall day, she was no longer picking up the phone. I called that morning—was it near noon? I hope she heard my voice on the machine before she left the house. (She was in Kentucky, and I was in Massachusetts; two months had passed since we last talked.) "I'll be driving all afternoon. Call me anytime."

I want to believe she paused, that she brightened, just one moment. But how could she have brightened when she was no longer picking up the phone, when she had written out a note, when she had tucked a bottle of pills into her pocket? She didn't change her mind. She took their dog for a walk to a wooded area. She didn't want her husband to have to find her. She wrote our names in black ballpoint on Post-its to affix to cardboard boxes she left for all of us: in mine, books, a key chain, a clutch of pomegranate-colored beads strung together like flowers, a clay plaque that says *create* in raised letters. Her husband handed me my box after the service. I keep the Post-it near me; I keep the plaque on a wall in my apartment—in every apartment I have lived in for the past nine years; I misplace the beaded flowers and find them again every few months. I called on a Friday morning. Her husband called me on Sunday. It had taken a day to find her.

I want to believe she heard my voice before she left the house. It is selfish, but I want to believe she knew I was thinking of her. Still, I will never know what she thought or if she heard or what she felt, at the end.

Once, crossing the street, we saw children. They cross the street with their teacher. They are a line of ducks in the rain. In my head, I am taking notes: *I passed children, walking like ducklings. They wore blue slickers and yellow boots.* Notes to myself, notes to LeeAnne. It has been nearly ten years now. My French dictionary is no help. I would like to find a word for this besides suicide, but in French the word is the same. I would like to find a word for a friend who was better than a friend, who was as close as a sister, but I do not have a sister (*une sœur*), and something in these words won't translate: to be like something is not the same as to be something. I would like a better word. Something to stay past this passing of time, something that will last.

Paris is for writers—for everyone who wants something from their wanting. What do you do in a city? You walk. I walked. Repetition is key. In my head, I sang. *Je te plumerai la tête.* I walked around the city for one week. (In my head, I spoke French.) I looked at the river. It rained. I must have looked at the river. *Alouette.* I walked and walked. I took pictures. *Skylark, lovely skylark.* I thought of a pool that once existed—rough concrete, paint chipping, the sharp comfort of chlorine. I thought of LeeAnne. We were markers, marking what? There was earth and it was sinking. *Et la tête.* Of how she just wanted to rest. *Et la tête.* Of what use is the head. There is ringing. Of what use is a ghost-blue pool. I am in my head. *Din din don.* And then ringing. *Din din don.* There is the outline of what was once a pool—now an indentation, now an impression, now fresh, now earth.

We should have been two girls, swimming. (I cannot say it in French.) We should have been two girls lying on the flagstones in the sun, talking, and lemon juice in our hair and iced tea in tall flowered glasses by a light blue pool; we would have had time. So this is the Seine. I know I should let her go. So this is time. I'm not ready yet. We are flowers alive by the side of the pool, bowing and bowing toward each other, heads bent, as girls always do.

[2011]

Bird

I have not been to Cobb's Hill since last summer, when I returned to Rochester for a wedding. I was with A. We had each flown in from the larger cities where we lived, and we were restless in our quiet town after each event ended. It was an Indian wedding; you had to pace yourself. We found ourselves on one of those nights parking on Highland after driving around and then hiking up the drive. Red radio tower lights blinking in the distance. It took on the quality of a date or of high school only after we began walking.

Sitting on our hill looking out at our city, we talked, the way you talk when you are looking at a skyline—any skyline— and it is warm enough, a particular kind of warm, which is not too hot, not too humid, not anything but enough to make you glad that your skin is the only layer between you and the world, heat-lightning in the distance, talking too much to people you don't know well enough. But no one is listening to anyone too closely. Overtalking. This was seventeen again. We listened to the sound of our own voices, heard them cross each other. We leaned into each other.

When my parents were young, when they were new transplants to this country, they brought their young children, my brother and me, to Cobb's Hill. And summer and fall evenings we would chase each other around the reservoir and race each other down the hill. My parents and their good friends, a childless couple—kind but frozen in that way of people without kids—would walk patiently, their after-dinner digestive. I always looked for the roof of the house with eight chimneys. As though I had a tic, I would count all eight and wonder the same thing: *Who lives there? How can you have eight chimneys?*

The house was one of many talismans for me, landmarks in the two or three miles of this city I still recognize as mine. The sky was a faint pink-purple, and you could even see the top of our high school from that hill. Now it surprises me to consider how many other people this park must belong to. I rarely went to the nonreservoir side of the park, where there are basketball courts and fountains and tennis courts. I don't play tennis. For me, Cobb's Hill is the reservoir, is the scrubby patch of pines and the clearing where people practice tai chi, is the cement structure, houselike, at the top where people sit with their kids or their lovers. And it is the hill where we went sledding or sat on for kissing. At the top, we'd always pause to look at the view. We would sit on the steps leading down from the pavilion and the gatehouse that looks like Greek or Roman ruins—something classical about the architecture, something dignified—though these columns were built in the 1900s and they are not in ruins.

Cobb's Hill felt like my backyard, the corner of the city and the suburbs, an intersection, a line. It was where we learned to drive, where we ran sprints in track practice. If you run again and again up and down the same hill, you will lose your breath. Pause at the foot of the hill, hands resting on your hips, you will look at the row of pine trees instead of the skyline, because that is what you can see, and you will begin to belong to a place and it will belong to you.

That summer night, I was walking with A. We strolled and paused behind a Canada goose that wasn't able to fly and just squawked in dismay to another goose, its friend, floating on the reservoir. It walked in front of us on the circular paved path surrounding the water, flapping its wings and hopping. And it was something, watching an animal that was never going to make it, this bird that had stopped being able to fly and would not clear the iron fence, wondering what was going to happen to it; and we were walking in the perfect night air, and though we liked each other and talked; we were back somehow in high school, powerless, driving around looking for a pizza place open past eleven.

We were never to kiss. We were only to look at the dark water, only to talk around and at, to nod at the three other people who were there on the hill at night, to stop a moment to lean into the bars around the reservoir and then to resume walking. He chased after the goose a bit—we wondered if we could scare it into flying. Startle it. It didn't seem right for a tall bird to be walking in front of us like a woman in shorts, exercising.

At the wedding, while waiting to get a drink at the bar, A and I had suddenly realized that almost everyone we had grown up with, and almost everyone there, was married. We were in our thirties, but it still surprised us. A lives in San Francisco.

I live in New York. In those places we are merely single, not odd.

I can see, at Cobb's Hill, my seventeen-year-old self with B before our first date. We were going to dinner at a place his mom had recommended, and it was spring but still cold. He picked me up at my house, and we stopped briefly at Cobb's Hill to look at the sunset. And I am nineteen, running down the hill the night we both knew it would never work out, and then in my early twenties with C, and he had brought a bottle of white wine and two glasses. He was always scaring me because he wanted to talk about things I didn't want to talk about.

It was winter again (it was nearly always winter then in Rochester), and when C and I got out of the car, B was there with his girlfriend. So we drank the wine and talked, but we also got out of the car and went sledding. It was a steep hill, and you could spill right out into traffic on Monroe, but that and the stories of people who had been paralyzed—they never stopped us. I shared a sled with B's girlfriend, one like me, whom he did not marry. I only remember that she had dark hair and one of us must have held onto the other in order to stay in the sled. B and C liked each other, too; we went out for beers once or twice at Rohrbach's.

A is for animal, B is for boy. We, all of us, were in our early twenties then. Who knew how any of it was going to turn out? We were young, each pair of us an animal. We were ourselves, fledgling: birds that would never lift off, never rise.

[2010]

Walking Tributaries

In his book about the Upper Iowa River, *Oneota Flow*, Decorah native David Faldet writes, "We are walking tributaries. The smell we sense in rain, in an ocean, or on the banks of a midwestern river attracts us because its familiarity runs deep." Iowa returns to me. I remember the view from the top of the hill where I lived. This was the Christiansons' home, the buttercream-colored house at 110 Pleasant Hill Road—a house with a Norwegian name—Soli Høgda or "Sunny Heights." I can feel the sun heating up the small square living room, warming my face and legs. Most days, I sat gazing from this perch at the First Lutheran Church steeple, the dark red brick of the old middle school, and the miniature downtown.

I drank my coffee or eight-dollar red wine and looked toward the center of town, which once held stunning river views before the river was rerouted to prevent flooding. The sky gathered streaks of pink and purple, deepened, and streetlights emerged on the downtown main street, Water Street. I stayed for nine months—enough time to create a new life or spend an academic year as writer-in-residence, renting the house of another professor.

♥

Three years later, I returned to that same small town, Decorah, for three weeks in the summer. I was without a car this time, and rented a bike in order to get from campus to town to the house where I stayed. Ben at Decorah Bicycles, next to The Whippy Dip, the local soft-serve ice cream place, took a brown Trek bike down from the racks. He was handsome in a blonde, midwestern, athletic way; were I ten years younger, I'd allow myself a ten-minute crush. Outside, he showed me the gears. "Remember, to change the gears you have to be pedaling," Ben said. *When have I ever felt this old?* He left me to push up onto the bike, to circle the parking lot like a seven-year-old boy, to find my balance. I concentrated on making circles and loops, remembering the freedom I felt when I first learned, late at ten years old, to ride a bike.

During that year in Iowa, I felt free, felt the flat edges of the world curl up against my fingers, pressed myself into the earth and felt, for a moment, held. Far from the ballast of family and familiar places, far from everywhere I had lived previously, I felt weightless, unanchored by the past. First it was startling, depressing. Then, I found my footing, finding the familiar in the unfamiliar.

When I returned to Decorah for the summer, I worked with a community-based collaborative dance company, Black Earth Arts. Leigh—fierce, athletic, unsentimental—took the time to memorize one of my poems. She read it with such feeling and intensity we were both brought to tears. She walked across the stage, moved through the words and the story they told about driving along the Mississippi. The words became current—a current—connecting me to someone I barely knew. She inhabited those words, and I believed them again; I believed in words and movement and how they can, briefly, elevate a moment from the past and deliver it to us again.

I am getting ready to move again, to leave New York, and water is what I will remember about New York City too—the East River's pungent brackish smell, the swirls and eddies, looking across to the lighthouse on the northern tip of Roosevelt Island, this view a few blocks away from where I live. When I am away from any place I have ever loved, it is the view of water that brings me back. I feel the desire to return to Iowa every summer. What I know how to do, what I love to do, is to walk through a landscape with the layers of every other time I've been there underneath and around me shifting as I walk. I am five years ago and now with every step. I am ten, balancing on two wheels, pedaling forward and then pedaling back to brake and then gliding before I realize I can ride, that I have been riding for two minutes when two minutes before I did not know how.

❧

In her essay "The Site of Memory," Toni Morrison writes,

> All water has a perfect memory and is forever trying to get back to where it was. Writers are like that: remembering where we were, what valley we ran through, what the banks were like, the light that was there and the route back to our original place. It is emotional memory—what the nerves and the skin remember as well as how it appeared. And a rush of imagination is our flooding.

As I write this, I am readying myself for a trip to India—a place so unfamiliar to me that the thought of going there sometimes makes my skin crawl. I have to remind myself to breathe, to pedal. I have to remind myself I've flown across two oceans to India twice before. I have to remind myself that it's okay to not know my parents' homeland, and that some memory runs in my bloodlines. I have to remind myself that once upon a time Iowa was unfamiliar, too.

[2011]

Castle, Fort, Lookout, House

It was not you I wanted; it was more than you. It was not a handsome man I asked for; it was love. However, I got a handsome man.

Your mother, a hippie, named you after rock. This is how I always thought of you, but I was wrong: you are the absence of rock.

Your eyes shine and two veins Braille your forehead. Your hair spreads outward like the sun. You are lit up; you glow—incandescent. You are one-sixteenth Indian you tell me, proudly. Did I care? No. You wonder if this is the source of your affinity with your Indian friends, with the Indian girlfriend who came before me. Is this infatuation or my heart?

You are half Jamaican, half Rochesterian; you are my heart. Does this mean my own heart does not love me? Why do we love beauty when it is not love?

A quarry is a large, deep pit or a type of open-pit mine. Quarries are often used for building materials. I wanted to build a castle, a fort, a lookout, a house. I did not intend to get stuck in an open-pit mine. Who intends these things?

One November night, I wanted to get back to Brooklyn from Washington Heights. I used to be scared of hailing cabs. "I'll go with you," you said. You hailed a black cab. "One drink," you said. Our friends fled. You hailed a yellow cab to Brooklyn. You got in the car with me, came up the stairs with me. You stayed.

People lie, they flatter; they are nice or they want to be. You lie, but you say it's not lying. You just don't tell me everything.

The last time I saw you, you looked past me—and this is what drew me to you. What has always drawn me to you. (Look out.)

It was not a boyfriend I asked for, it was a husband. It was not a husband I asked for, it was love. It was not a place to swim I needed but a place to rest. It was not someone perfect I asked for, it was a songbird like you, with your hair sticking straight up, your wolfish teeth, your golden eyes. And though I had been on my way out the door in Washington Heights, I turned around. I dropped my coat. I stayed. With you, I will always want to stay.

Nine years have passed since that night in Washington Heights.

My name means water. You are the absence of rock: something that can hold water, something that is whole without it.

Why do we love beauty, when it is not love, not at all?

There is a second definition of quarry: an animal pursued by a hunter, hound, predatory mammal, or bird of prey. A thing or person that is chased or sought.

I wanted a castle, a fort, a lookout, a house. I did not want the absence of rock.

Water-filled quarries are deep, often fifty feet or more. This water is often bitterly cold. It was not a fool I asked for. Am I a fool? This want. This is not a fort. A fort is if someone needs protection. Who needs protection? A water-filled quarry is a swimming hole. My name means pure water. You shock me sometimes, still. I shock myself, too. It was not a handsome man I asked for. My unwillingness to extract myself. It was love.

Nine years have passed since that night in Washington Heights. *Black cab, yellow cab, castle, fort.* You, swimming away from me. Love. You, turning toward me in the bed, light slanting in from the streetlamps, through the latticed window, from the coming sunrise, from the day.

[2011]

Curriculum

AREA STUDIES

The map was printed on a handkerchief. It is a map of a place that no longer exists. *British East Africa*. On a handkerchief— you can hold the Republic of Tanganyika near your nose! Around the carved-out section of Africa float pictures, symbols: a rhinoceros, a bird you cannot identify. Strangely, we had two maps, nearly identical, except that the print on the handkerchiefs, the outlines of the place, were slightly blurry; neither was perfect. I was always thinking about stretching these handkerchiefs, ironing them, framing them for a present for our mother who was from there, but nothing came of that. I was a child who wanted perfect. They were hers, so it would have been giving something of hers back to her; what kind of gift is that? A good one or a sad one, or both? I never did it. I still find them from time to time.

WOMEN'S STUDIES

Three embroidered, cream-colored cloths—or are they two— float in the kitchen. They are not framed the way stitching, cross-stitching, and needlepoint are framed in other people's front hallways and parlors and living rooms and above stairs. They are not framed at all. They are not letters, pilgrim blue.

They are not a repetition of vowel sounds, of consonants. They do not linger. They are flowers, and they curl. They taunt me: what was it that I meant to do? *To frame, to frame, to hang up.* Nothing done. Were they part of what women had to do to show some sort of mastery over the smallest surface? I will never embroider like that. We had latch hook, just hours of watching *The Guiding Light* and *All My Children* and hooking. The ugliest designs and colors until some design, oversize red and blue mushrooms in a field, grew, moldlike, in shag rug splendor.

VISUAL STUDIES

My friend Anne says, "Use the old frames and wear them. Replace the lenses." I, too, wear glasses. This is one way I know I belong to my family since I don't really resemble them. They are my mother's cat-eye glasses, from the sixties, or maybe it was the seventies. They are broken, and I cannot bear to get rid of them. I keep them in the blue-and-white flowered glasses case she always used. I keep them in a wooden box that says *Buffalo Baking Powder Company* that I bought one summer at an antique fair. I was not even twenty-five. What did I know then of the way things break down? Of the way I would and one day did? I want to believe I will wear her glasses one day. I keep thinking about these objects that have no particular use, how I study them: two handkerchief maps of an area now called something else; pale, needle-pointed flowers (unframed); spectacles with black and gold rims, a relic signifying forthcoming absence, these glasses of a mother I will lose one day.

[2012]

Your Wilderness Is Not Permanent

"I think we'd like to make love now." The words repeated: a murmur, a shimmer, a cat walking across covers. The woman saying these words had red hair and very pale skin. She wore sparkly eyeliner, purple. She lay next to a man beneath a brown sleeping bag. It seemed like a reasonable request. My eyes flickered open. I looked at their bare shoulders and collarbones. (*Why were they saying this to me?*) The night, absent of stars, wound itself around us. I lay curled near their blanket-covered legs. I closed my eyes and fell back to sleep.

I opened my eyes. The night lifted, a navy-blue scrim rising. The white man had dreads. The white woman told me that she had been a sixth-grade teacher. "I was a teacher, too," I said. The man grinned. He reminded me of a former student who often argued with me and liked to talk. A lot. My student was tall but hunched over, always wore an olive-colored jacket, and something about him seemed oddly animal-like, but not in an unpleasant way. I paused. Then: "What am I doing in your car?"

"I dropped acid," I said, "but the guy I was with—I made him promise that I would get home okay." (*I'm going to kill him, I thought. This is not okay.*) "And I don't have a ride out of here. I'm stuck."

"It's okay," they said. "You're fine. Burning Man is a safe place. It's different than the outside world." They laughed and said, "It's a story. You'll find a ride. But we really would like to make love now."

I opened the door of the SUV. The cold air, the sun breaking at the horizon, long rays, long shadows. I did not want to leave the car's nest but knew it was not cool to keep two people at Burning Man from having sex. I did not know where I was in relation to my camp. I was afraid of being lost, I was mortified things had gotten—that I had gotten—out of control. I was in the desert with no way out. "We woke up," they said, "and there you were."

♥

I don't remember much about that night except that the temperature dropped in the desert once the sun set. If I am cold, there is almost nothing I will not do to get warm again, including breaking into a strange car close to midnight. I do remember this: hundreds of points of light lit the inky darkness, glittering until the dust storm arose. The night sky stretched, yawning to show the Milky Way's silvery ellipse, an elongated spirograph, spinning. Stars shot out here and there, crisscrossing the sky. We snapped on light sticks as bracelets, as chokers—slender bands of fluorescent yellow, green, red, blue, orange. We biked toward the art structures, blazing in the darkness: the figure of a woman arching, hands clasped in a balletic pose, the temple outlined in the bright colors of Christmas tree lights, almost winking. We rode through swirls of dust until the outlines of art structures appeared, magic, lit up against the dusty night sky. And then

I was by myself. I was alone. I didn't know where my camp was; I could not locate anything, no landmarks. I didn't recognize myself but for the desperate attempt to vanquish the cold—my personal kryptonite. The cold makes it hard to stay within the contours of your own skin.

When I realized I had been sleeping next to strangers—on top of their blankets, curled in their bed, that I had broken into their car—I began to cry.

I climbed out of the cocoon of their car. "Don't forget your hat," the sparkly-lidded woman said. I stepped out into the waning nighttime sky, a violet haze, clutching my white wool hat. The blazing sun just rising in the desert, the morning sun roaring up, then clearing the horizon. I didn't have a watch on me. It was cold out, frigid even. I blinked, trying to see with dried-out contacts, to orient myself and find my way back to my camp and tent.

Months later, when I tell this story to my friend, Magda, she says, "I bet they've been telling this story to their friends, too."

♥

Burning Man comes with its own survival guide. That should have been a clue as to what lay ahead, but it only made me more curious to see why people went, and why they kept returning. The survival guide states, "Burning Man takes place in the beautiful, remote and inhospitable Black Rock Desert of Nevada . . . you are responsible in every regard for your own survival, safety, comfort, and well-being." The Man: an effigy burning, sharp flames flaring, engulfing, releasing the old year's demons, smoke against the black-blue sky, then fireworks, shooting curved lines into the sky. The flames leap higher, he collapses, a shout rises, a cheer; only night and darkness to witness. I missed it, but this is what I imagine, what other people described. I had promised to work at another retreat center, and it meant leaving early, before the Man burned. The festival occurs every August, the week prior to and through Labor Day weekend. It's not great timing for a teacher. It's terrible. Did they plan it this way?

Whether or not the timing was intentional, the fact is that I was not teaching for the first time in years. I was there. In Nevada. For me, Burning Man was a week of exceptions: I ate bacon that week. (I am a vegetarian. Normally.) I dropped acid (twice, the same night) and then remembered almost nothing about it. I'd never done anything outside of alcohol and pot—nor had I had much curiosity. I came of age in the Reagan era: Just Say No. I had done just that. I was thirty-nine, a month away from my next birthday. I had lost my job, had moved back in with my family. I was lost—not just on the Playa, but in my life.

♥

Before the morning I woke up in a stranger's SUV, I strapped on motorcycle goggles and rode a too-small mountain bike through that nighttime dust-and-wind storm in the desert. Later, I found out it was the kind of evening that made many people decide to stay in their tents. The four people I camped with snapped on light sticks, suited up, ventured out, and took acid. I did it too, but didn't mean to. "Just try it," they said. They handed me their extra light sticks, not just as costume or decoration but so other riders could see me in that dusty, windy darkness. They dropped acid. I thought I would say no. They had a pack of sugar cubes and handed me two. I took them. (What was I thinking?)

We rode through this mysterious moonscape studded with lit-up large-scale art installations, each of the structures emerging from the dust only as we approached. We pointed ourselves toward one in particular: the temple, made of ornate, filigreed wood, papered inside with hand-written messages, letters, pleas, prayers, photographs, eulogies for people who had passed, wishes for forgiveness. The temple radiated power, resonance, sadness, weight.

♥

The crowning event and spectacle of the festival is a large bonfire, in which the figure of a man is burned. I did not witness the burn. Other art is also created and then burned: ephemeral art. A city of nearly fifty thousand, Black Rock City, amasses for this week. You must bring your own water, your own food, a bike, costumes. I had never been to a festival of this size—a music festival or any kind of festival. Who were all of these people who hauled their own water and food to a festival? I couldn't understand the appeal.

The ten principles of Burning Man are radical inclusion, gifting, decommodification, radical self-reliance, radical self-expression, communal effort, civic responsibility, leaving no trace, participation, and immediacy. Radical self-reliance: "Burning Man encourages the individual to discover, exercise and rely on his or her inner resources." Did I rely on my inner resources? I did. Did I ask too much of my campmates? I did. I haven't asked them; they haven't said.

♥

School was a system I understood. But I struggled as a teacher. I was good with students but felt defeated at the end. I began to hate it. Months before I would have applied for tenure, my contract was not renewed. The first big failure in my life: humiliating, public, irreversible. Though I had been thinking about leaving, the letter stunned me and shocked my friends and colleagues.

No job, some unemployment benefits. I left New York, traveled for three months in India, my own eat pray love, studying yoga, staying with friends and relatives. Then I moved home. No regular job allowed me the opportunity to travel. I planned to work on a project with a friend in Seattle, stay with my uncle in the Bay Area, and work for a month in Big Sur. In Oakland, with three days to prepare, I decided to go to Burning Man.

♥

Burning Man runs on a gift economy. I was not prepared. The only gifts I carried with me were a bottle of gold nail polish and artisanal salted caramels wrapped in parchment paper, bought from a farmer's market in Columbia City, Seattle. I left a small brown box of them with the Oakland couple who shared their shade structure with me. They made coffee and bacon and shared that with us, too.

The one caramel I had put in my pocket made it through the laundry without melting over everything. At the laundromat, a woman approached me and said, "Where are you going?" I managed to croak out, "I've been camping." I could still barely speak, but I had spread out my clothes at the laundromat as I washed both my bags and clothes; dust and sweat coated everything. She said, "I'm reading a book about a woman who is camping"—and brought out a hardback book with a single hiking boot on the cover. *Wild.*

This heartened me. I'd met the writer and taught one of her essays, "The Love of My Life," for years. It was an essay my students and I loved. It was an essay that sometimes brought me to tears, even in class. Nothing I had done seemed as brave as her journey; still, I was flattered to be put in that category of adventure, of nerve. I think this is what I had wanted all along—to strengthen my nerve.

I did not show this woman what I had carried in my backpack: the program guide for Burning Man—just as thick as one for an academic conference.

"What Where When: Fertility 2.0." On the cover, a photo of pink synapses and what looks like coral, organic material. When I flipped through the guide, I saw some of the various offerings:

Naked Pub Crawl
Grateful Dyed
Mass Unicycle Ride
Clarity and Sex: Negotiating Sex on the Playa

Geology of the Black Rock Desert
Past Life Regressing Meditation
Human Energy System Healing
3rd Annual Healthy Friction Circle Jerk

I was just trying to hitch a ride.

♥

Here is the beginning: before we left Berkeley and drove toward the desert, Cinque said, "Do you know other people there? Because maybe you should get in touch with them, too." Cinque had found me the ticket to Burning Man. His question should have clued me in. It did, but I still wanted to go. I was in California; I was not, for the first time in nearly a decade, preparing classes for the fall semester. I was adrift. I did know people in Black Rock City but had no way to get in touch with them without texting or phone. And we were camped in the periphery, far from Center Camp, which had a ride share center.

Cinque has skin the same color as mine, green eyes, parents of different races, a disarmingly beautiful smile, and a temper he is quick to lose. I met him at a meditation center in Massachusetts, when we both worked in the kitchen. By the time we left, I had developed a minor crush.

On a quiet street in Berkeley, we packed and repacked the cars. The light was falling, orange and pink streaking the sky; we could hear the people across the street on their terrace or roof deck grilling, glasses clinking, laughter. They shouted to us, "Burning Man?" "Yeah," we hollered back. "Have a great burn!" they said. They returned to their grilling and drinking.

I half-wished I was on a deck with my own friends, staying. Cinque was riding with Leah, a woman he had met on a ride share board. He had secured me a place with his friend, John, who needed someone to share gas money. Cinque told me Leah was going to leave on Saturday, before the Man burned, and I could get a ride back with her.

Leah adjusted something on her bike with bike tools. She was in her early twenties and unfriendly. Before we climbed into our cars, I asked Leah if she was leaving Saturday like Cinque said, and if I could go back to Oakland with her. Leah said, "I'm not leaving until Sunday, after the Man burns." I can't remember now if Cinque was in hearing distance of this conversation or if I approached him after and told him. This is where everything gets fuzzy, slow-motion. The last light disappearing, night and stars emerging, a beneficent moon rising. Cinque said nothing.

It was the moment for me to pull out, but I had dropped two hundred on a ticket and another hundred on food and supplies. I had asked my uncle's downstairs tenant for a ride to Berkeley. I had borrowed an old boyfriend's sleeping bag (Chris had made a special trip to drop it off at my uncle's house). Chris said, "Don't do any drugs." I said, "I won't!" and shot him an eye roll. "I'm not interested in that."

I had bought a case of water and a sack of oranges at Costco and packages of prepared food from Trader Joe's. I had bought the last package of baby wipes from a Walgreens in Oakland, which I stopped into with my childhood friend, Anne. She suggested the wipes, and also lent me her headlamp. She had been to Burning Man many times but was taking a break. It seemed too late to back out, to call up my uncle and go home loaded with sacks of oranges, apples, water, and a sleeping bag and headlamp I no longer needed. I decided to be hopeful and maneuvered myself into the blue Honda. Where else is there to go but forward?

♥

I found a way out. At the end, when I was in our far-off camp, a light blue Prius crept toward us. Aviva, whom I met at a camp devoted to dance, helped me haul my two backpacks and sleeping bag over to the car. I left food, my bike, a bottle of wine, and garbage for my campmates to contend with. I was leaving Burning Man before the Man burned. ("I don't know, I don't know, I don't know," I said.)

I didn't know if I should go with Nate, camping next to us, who had also decided he was going to leave before the Man burned. He created video games, seemed nice, we had even attended the same state university. But I had the sense as though he was looking for something, and I didn't want to drive many miles and stay in a hotel room halfway to Oakland to find out what it was he was searching for.

"I don't know, I don't know, I don't know," I murmured, even while we pulled away from the camp. I was in the car and Aviva was driving. I decided to go with her. I didn't know if it was the right decision. And then I was asleep for a long time, those drugs, no sleep, relief. Twice, on our way to the Bay Area, there were no bathrooms and we pulled over. I unfolded myself from the front seat, dashed to the side of the road, untied my drawstring pants and squatted. Weeks later, Aviva said she didn't realize how out of character that was for me.

These days, when I am far from the heat and confusion and sweat and exile of Burning Man, when I am wondering when I will find my next job, a partner, a place to live, I remember driving down my street on my way to the store or to the gym and pulling over. It was WDKX, the local urban station. There was a preacher preaching (it was Sunday morning) and he said, once and again and again: Your wilderness is not permanent. Your Wilderness Is Not Permanent. There were capitals in his words. All capitals. YOUR WILDERNESS IS NOT PERMANENT.

I was so scared in the desert, without friends, unable to reach anyone, a phone drained of power, a spirit without charge, and so many things in those days seemed hopeless: finding my way around Black Rock City, having enough water in my water bottle, enough sunblock on my face, enough food, energy bars; a bandana against the dust storm, a program guide, being present enough that I could find my way home. I stopped worrying about the fact that I had failed. I regret not taking more pictures, but the desert demanded I stay present.

Cinque said, when I talked to him a few months later, "You manifested that situation when you worried about things. You made things difficult for yourself by worrying. I knew you would be able to get out of there okay." I thought he might apologize for the misinformation. There was no apology.

"I had nothing but good intentions," he said. "I knew you wanted to go," he said, "and I did what I could do to make it happen." That was true; he did. I almost didn't see the beauty at Burning Man—the pageantry, the terrifying spectacle of biking in a wind and dust storm, the enormous desert night sky, the exhilaration because I was so worried.

At any particular moment, your wilderness, wild as it is, is not permanent. We danced and kissed, and rode our bikes around the desert, tripping. Cinque and me, apparently (he tells me; I have only a vague memory). I ventured beyond what I had seen or done before, not knowing enough to pay the fee to camp with a larger, organized camp with meal plan options. I wanted to see what brought people back to Burning Man again and again. I wanted to go beyond what I knew. I wanted to break some rules.

I was angry at Cinque for promising me a way home that did not exist, and I was angrier at myself for getting in the car at all when I could have eaten the price of the ticket and stayed in Berkeley. I wanted to be like the free spirits and pot dealers I've known; I wanted to just go. All my life, I have been biking with brakes on.

We want to be able to move. We want to be able to do what we want to do. I wanted to go to Burning Man and needed to get to Big Sur after, which I had planned my whole year around. I wanted to see the spectacle. Maybe the dust and sparkle would rub off on me, maybe I would strengthen my nerve, maybe I would learn to have some balance, to ride out my anxiety; maybe I would coast.

Instead, I forgot to take my antidepressants, drank scotch, took acid, and had no way home.

♥

In the only pictures I have from my four days at Burning Man, I am wearing a black T-shirt with the words "Savage Beauty" written in white letters. The shirt references the title of the biography of the poet Edna St. Vincent Millay; it was part of a fundraiser for a writer's colony in Upstate New York. No one who saw me in the desert would have known that. I had not brought anything with me that looked particularly savage. I knew I was no savage beauty. I was just brown. It started to feel like a bad joke. I left the T-shirt in California.

Now I wish I had taken it. I wanted to be both savage and beautiful—what woman doesn't? I felt neither in the desert; the desert was both. I was both, too, but who knows that kind of thing at the time? I was more accustomed to writers sitting around in idyllic retreats than radical self-reliance. I want to say I found a fierceness in myself—but did I? I found some sort of hidden nerve to bike miles in the blazing sun to find a way to leave. I talked myself out of panicking when alone in the night and darkness.

It's some months later, but I am still thinking about what being there meant. Was it okay to ask for such a big favor—eight hours out of her way—from someone I had just met? I did it. Was it okay to break into someone's car? I did that, too. I was no longer living in New York. I had moved back to my sad upstate city. I had left the epicenter. I wanted to burn. I wanted to be free.

Many years ago, I spent a week in Paris. I thought I would visit the Louvre and the Eiffel Tower. I went to the Centre Pompidou and the Musée d'Orsay but not the Louvre. I did not see the *Mona Lisa*; I did not climb the Eiffel Tower either. I went to the desert for Burning Man and did not see the Man burn—the culmination, the catharsis, the highlight, the point. It was me burning, my old self, that I had been after all along. I wanted to shake it loose, my old ways, rules, teaching. I was a phoenix; I wanted to burn. I was a circle of stars, silver in the night sky. It was me: I was the spectacle in the desert I had traveled so far to see.

[2012, 2019]

Deluxe

ONE

She is the last of her siblings who is alive; Mother says she is tired. (Ba will never say she is tired.) Ba is my mother's mother. She walks, leaning on the walker, from one side of the basement, the foot of the stairs, to the bar at the other end. This is exercise. There is a wet bar with its own sink and no drinks. (A bar in the basement: it was a ranch house of a certain era.) Fluorescent tube lights, white and red. Stickers of sexy ladies tattoo the walls, a remnant of previous owners, thirty-five years ago; the decals still glow, voluptuous pinups, Marilyn Monroe, Rita Hayworth, spilling out of their green and red silk camisoles and chocolate-brown fur stoles, sitting with legs crossed or lounging on one hip. Across from the bar sits the pantheon of Hindu gods and goddesses, Krishna, Laxmi, Ram-Laxman-Sita-Hanuman-the-monkey-god, Ganesh-the-elephant-god, Shiva and his trident, purple and magnificently furious. To be magnificently furious! The occasional background holy cow. The pictures show no children except a blue baby Krishna, scooping butter from a clay pot, but I know that many of them, these gods and goddesses, are parents.

TWO

Children are hanging off the bars. One child sits on a leather platform; another child pushes the walker. The platform is a shelf with no discernible use. We need things that have no discernible use. These children belong to me; they are my nephews. I like to use the word "my." Children monkey bar across the walker—no, not really, but they are monkeys, they are squirrels, they are boys who love cars. They are boys: they love motion. They twist, shout, change direction, repeat, repeat. They push their great-grandmother's walker across the kitchen floor in a spacious, five-bedroom, nineties-built home in eastern Massachusetts decorated with luxe European antiques, not far from water.

For these boys, everything spins, everything is a toy, wheels equals toy equals theirs. They appeared on a hot August day, nearly seven years ago, in a hospital in Boston, C-sectioned from their mother's abdomen. For them, scooters, skateboards, bicycles, four-wheeler motorized car, motion and mobility and running away from me and from each other, matters. Yet another set of boys, with wheels or without them, running in the opposite direction. "Chase me," they shout. "Get me," they say. "Gonna get me?" they ask hopefully, they implore.

THREE

It's a Cruiser Deluxe Classic Walker with Detachable Flip Back. My grandmother has one at our home. My father uses a simple metal one at the hospital. Prostate cancer. Everyone gets it, but still, we were surprised. They say doctors make the worst patients. My mother (not a doctor) says they are right. He would rather be home, he would rather be at work, but wouldn't everyone? No one likes hospitals, but not everyone signs up to work in one. I watch him lean on the simple walker, and the cords and fluid bags trail him like confetti. They are tiny children trying to outrun themselves, or even tinier ones, determined—and shrill—to nurse.

FOUR

You will use this for your knee replacements, your hip replacements, your heart when one of the boys you chased (not remembering they are supposed to chase you) breaks your heart. You stopped eating for weeks. You hung your handwashing off the bars to dry—the periwinkle blue bra you bought at a tiny store on the Upper East Side and the only lace-edged black silk underwear you ever owned. You were embarrassed that you bought beautiful underwear for a man who found you, at best, likable, who refused to say "love." "I like you, " he would say. "Hey cutie. " And somehow this didn't make you sad or angry for years. (Now, once angry, you don't know how to stop.) Who was that person? And was she, though in her twenties, already limping along behind a cart of broken bones?

FIVE

At the front of the big box store, next to the mall, they are lined up, to the side, congregating; they are parishioners after church. Strollers, walkers, canes, crutches, walking sticks.

The cane displays a curved metal handle and is propped against the wall next to a single crutch. They are restless, ladies waiting outside for their sons to finish karate, nursing a cup of coffee. They are parents leaning on the fence at summer soccer, waving to their children, exchanging sangria recipes. But where are the people? The mall has eaten them up, swallowed them alive as malls do. Mostly they return, but burdened now by packages, brown paper bags, clothes with tags, more things they heap on the strollers or hang from the walkers or the wide red and gray shopping carts, which also loiter near the entrances and exits, waiting for trouble.

SIX

If you have a child, when you are old you will have someplace to walk your walker: a smooth place. I have no children. I don't know when the irreversible collapsing will begin (it has already begun). The shortening, the shrinking, the pulling back into itself, the declaring, the rusting out, the turning. Where will I walk my walker? (Black, ridged plastic handles, smooth metal bars, a corruptible body, heavily leaning?) I am afraid to imagine fluorescent lights and white tiled floors, cool and patient and horrifying, a hospital or facility, assisted living, but I can imagine it anyway. I imagine it anyway. I should be doing other things (at this age), but I take the time to imagine it, anyway.

[2012]

Thank You

You will never know me, will never know your father once professed (many times, over a few months, the way boys will) to love me; will not know the first time we made love you were in your bedroom next door sleeping, and we paused to listen when we heard you (I worried, unused to this situation) call out in sleep.

Your father showed me pictures of you in a pale pink leotard and translucent white skirt, a series capturing your curly hair and sparkly eyes, and assured me you'd love me. But you will never meet me now, and I will never meet you, though I heard months of stories about you and gave you two books, both of which I heard you loved.

One was a small blank book I made at a community bindery, stitching the seam, knotting the thread—the first one I had ever made. I brought the book to our first date, blind. You told your father something he said he'd never heard you say before: *I love this book so much I'm not going to say thank you.* I wonder now—from whom did your father say the books came?

After returning from a friend's Mardi Gras Vodka Baby Shower in New York, I saved a string of shiny purple beads to give to you, guessing from your dance recital pictures you might like them, maybe even love them. But I don't think he gave them to you. I'm guessing, though.

The first time your father and I went away for the weekend, I was surprised to see your car seat in the back, the legion of stickers festooning your window. I was surprised by my surprise. Although I never met you, you were everywhere.

The last time I saw your father he was looking out his apartment window to make sure I reached my car. "Text me," he had said, "when you get home." He wanted to know I was safe. Snow upstate, night driving, can be treacherous. This is the last thing he ever said to me.

I will never have the chance to love you, to be your dad's annoying girlfriend or your evil stepmother or your big sister or your babysitter or your sort-of friend.

I broke up with him that night, frustrated at living in the small space between your bedtime and his; disappointed at not meeting you, at not being invited (rather, uninvited) to meet your grandmother, the famous Connecticut writer. "Let's at least try," I later wrote in an email message, sent hastily the night after I ended things. I wrote: "I miss you and I love you."

Maybe he loved me so much, your father, that he decided he would also not say thank you and also never reply. He had eyes that shone when he talked about you and also when he looked at me, across a low-lit restaurant table covered with oyster shells and chardonnay, his favorite, you know. "Thank you for loving me," he once said to me. We had marveled, then, at our good luck. I drank chardonnay, too, to match, though it's not my favorite. I hoped I might someday count, though not as much as you—never as much as you (that's not what I wanted, either).

Now I wonder about the woman who came before me (there's always one who comes before you; can I at least tell you that?), the one he left your mother for. She was young, younger than me, in her twenties, on her way to becoming a high-powered lawyer in DC, and also never met you. He told me he loved her, too. And that she broke up with him, too.

Did she study your doll stroller, parked in the corner of the living room, and tiny, shockingly pink shoes, strewn in the stark, gray foyer? Did she also stoop to help fold your star-patterned pajamas and sturdy purple underwear, your tiered dresses and miniature leggings? So many ruffles, so many kinds of pink, so many things. And did she also wonder if someday she might be a mother, maybe even a step, but still someone to whom you sometimes don't say thank you, even when you know you should?

[2013]

365 Pelham Road

Ranch houses, when I was growing up, were not cool. At least in my mind, at least on that street, in the 1980s. People appreciate them now—or maybe it's just everyone's eventual knee problems. My neighborhood displays an odd mix of housing styles along its streets. The developers ran out of money, I read, during the Depression. By the time people were building again, well after World War II, styles had changed. Thus, ranch houses live next to Tudors, split-levels next to Colonials.

My life is a ranch house—laid out squarely, not coyly, in levels like the Colonial homes on the street. No dormer windows or dreamy second-story verandas or slight, whimsical balconies in my house. No attic bedroom or interesting third story. I am straightforward, to a fault, often without decoration.

Sometimes I think I am uncomplicated, but I know it's not true. Ranch houses have their hidden spaces and places, too, even if they are not as old, not as interesting, not as layered as the fake Tudors and the Capes; they suggest a vision of family I could never quite get behind. Ranches present a large formal living room with picture windows and wide, open spaces. Pictures of a happy family. I never wanted anyone to be able to see into my home—houses are for hiding, a place to be invisible, to be visible and legible only to yourself, a place to read and restore.

The only other house my parents owned before that was also a ranch house. (They are, at any rate, consistent.)

At least we had an interesting added-on room—the blue room—a mother-in-law attachment. I am the addition, the mother-in-law attachment. I am not a mother-in-law; I am a returned child, boomeranging back every five or ten years. I think about the woman for whom it was built, this room with its own bathroom and a walk-in closet and a cedar closet and four bright windows framing two corners across three sides of the room. It has the feel of a sun porch. I must think about her weekly since I moved back here, and how kind (or necessary) it was for the Lemperts, the people who built the home, to do that for the parent who moved in with them. Everyone needs a little space.

One of the original owners asked to see the house once, years after they had moved, and my mother said no. It upset me when I heard this; I would want to be allowed back in if or when we move from the house, leave this house, lose this home.

Did he or she just ring the doorbell one day? I imagine it that way.

When I ask her about it again, my mother does not remember the previous owners stopping by at all. Did I make up the memory out of fear? That someday this won't be my house.

This I know: this house meant something once, to people other than us.

We talk about the house a lot, still. We live here, still, my parents and me, now joined by my grandmother. My parents were grateful for it—the location, the large finished basement that doubled as a meeting place for their community. Pujas, bhajans, Hindu festivals, lectures, poetry readings, visiting swamis. On those nights, their friends' cars lined the street and their shoes filled the garage. We kids played hide-and-seek or freeze tag, swarmed around the house, or swam. In those days, we had a pool.

I often wished my house sat closer to Highland, which bisects Pelham Road, or that we lived on Upper Pelham, which is what I called the other (older, stately, more elegant) half of the street between Highland and East. A ranch would have been out of place on that side. And I wonder about that now—my almost-obsession with the houses on the street. They seem almost like old friends or parents of friends—I have known their faces for so long, over so many years. Thirty-five years of driving by the same houses, walking by the same houses, years of disembarking from a yellow school bus and trudging home on uneven cement sidewalks. It's an old enough neighborhood that the sidewalks buckle and grass grows between squares.

I orient myself from that house. Number 365: the number of days in a year, we would tell our friends—that's how to tell our house apart from the other tan ranch houses at the end of the street. Even though the bedrooms, like everything in a ranch, are on the first floor, I always felt safe. Both the bedroom in which I grew up and the bedroom in which I now live, the mother-in-law attachment, face the backyard. And I value that—the solidity and privacy of the house. A fort, for keeping the world outside at bay. I knew if a job ended, I could always come back. There was a place for me. I called it my house, still, though I hadn't lived there in years, had in fact lived in other states. Maybe I always knew I would be back. I think I did. I think I always knew.

[2013]

There Is No Mike Here

In 1970-something, some kid from the neighborhood came knocking at the door: "Can Mike come out to play?"

"Mike?" My mom asked. "There is no Mike here."

And then my brother pushed out from behind her. "I'm Mike," he said. And he went out to play.

I was too young to remember this, but it is a story I know in the retelling. When my mother tells the story, though she laughs, I can still hear the shock and dismay, the register of hurt and bewilderment in her voice—that he would even have thought to change his name. *Samir*. She had to leave him in India with my grandparents when she and my father came to the United States to work in 1967. My parents weren't told that once they started the green card application process, they wouldn't be able to leave the United States, and my brother wouldn't be able to join them. They didn't see him for three years while they waited for their green cards and then applied for his. Samir's name means wind—and this name is something my mother gave him.

I attended an elementary school outside Rochester, New York, called Council Rock, referring to a treaty made by the white settlers with the Seneca Indians. The white folks broke the treaty and named a school instead. These are the Indians we studied. The Iroquois Confederacy—that was our nation.

These are the Indians I grew up thinking about. I did not set foot in India until I was nineteen. I have never visited Uganda, where my mom was born, nor Kenya, where she grew up. As is true of any writer, I wrote poems then about what I thought about: how to locate, claim, or create what or who is home—how you learn where and to whom you belong. It is still what I think about obsessively.

Names carry, influence, and even define one's identity. Or sometimes we work in opposition to our names. I named one of my nephews Anand. I insisted on it—the paternal aunt's customary right to name—and I wanted a recognizably Indian name. My brother resisted: "Americans will mispronounce it and call him An-And. Not Ah-nund. I don't want him to be made fun of." He's right—some mispronounce it— but I wanted that name. Anand means happiness, and I had no greater wish for my nephew than for him to be full of joy, to be content.

My mother spells out the name of our street. (She has to do it. She has an accent.) *P as in Pineapple, E as in Elephant, L as in Larry, H as in Harry, A as in America, M as in Mary.*

I was married this year, and the nearly universal assumption that I would change my name startled and then irritated me. I *have* a name. My husband's name is not my name. His name is South Indian, as is he. Singaravelu is far more unusual than my surname—would this make me seem unique, and therefore more valuable, to an editor? Would it give me better Google search results? (The answer to the last question is yes.) Google my name and you will find a gaggle of doctors: the dermatologist I was once mistaken for when an editor wrote to me with skin care questions; the actress/dentist in

New York; the (male) cinematographer in Bombay; the radiologist in Boston, who also owns a yoga studio (we were in a class together in college).

In Ahmedabad or Edison, my name might as well have been Sarah Smith—it's that common a Gujarati name for women of my generation. But in western New York, it was always a topic of conversation: "What an unusual name!" "What does it mean?" "I love it!" Or: "That's stupid. It sounds like Bagel. Or Rachel. Or Angel." "Why is it spelled that way?" I knew what they meant when they said "unusual." I understood I was unusual because of the person asking me the question, not because I am unusual—every person is.

♥

"Through the Eyes of the Dark-Eyed Americans" is the title of the first poem I published, when I was sixteen. My high school literary magazine, edited by other serious, long-haired students who loved 10,000 Maniacs and gathered in the windowless office next to our cafeteria, chose it. Our magazine, called *Galaxy*, seemed to me to be just that—we were out there away from the cheerleaders, the future business leaders, and the rest of the East Coast even, but for me, it was everything, this world of words. I was not an editor, but I was on staff; we called ourselves "Galactites." The discussions were not unlike those I would later encounter in workshops in graduate school, but people were kinder, the stakes lower. We looked at poems blind. I was one of two or three nonwhite kids at the meetings. Years after, I wondered if everyone assumed "Through the Eyes of the Dark-Eyed Americans" was mine.

Hanging Loose, a Brooklyn-based literary magazine that devotes a section of every issue to poets of high school age, also published the poem. Later, Hanging Loose Press (connected with the journal) selected my poem for inclusion in *Bullseye*, an anthology of high school poetry. Hanging Loose is also the same press that published Sherman Alexie's first book. My poem had legs! "Through the Eyes of the Dark-Eyed Americans" placed in a countywide literary contest run by the downtown public library in Rochester. (I won fifty dollars, had my name in the local paper, and was taken out to lunch with the other winners at a fancy restaurant.) Even my parents' friends, other Indians, knew I was a poet—everyone read the paper. My *name* was in the paper. I existed! The poem placed in six other literary competitions. I have never again won so many awards for one piece of writing. My poem was good—and not because of its title alone or because of my name. (I've kept these records for all these years, as though I needed evidence to say the above, to make the claim I am a writer.)

Here are the first two verses:

Once,
for once
I would like to see the world
Through your eyes.

Is it a different place
With green or blue irises?
Are perceptions different?
Can you see me—
—me as i see myself?

Yes, I used the e. e. cummings "i." (Remember, I was in high school). Someone told me (a friend? an editor? a teacher? all of the above?) he/she had assumed that the speaker in the poem was me. Why? If you have a recognizably Indian name and brown skin does it automatically disqualify you from writing a persona poem? My college professor, Frank Bidart (white, male, American), published a now well-known poem in the voice of Ellen West, an anorexic woman living in Europe who died at thirty-three from her illness. That did not seem to be a problem.

I remember writing "Through the Eyes of the Dark-Eyed Americans." It appeared in nearly finished form—an easy labor that for me almost never happens. I didn't know then that poem was a gift. (I am still laboring over this essay.) I was sixteen. But I was also thinking back to when I was seven and spent second grade in California. I loved our textbook so much that my teacher gave me a copy before I moved back to New York. I'm holding it now. *Paths to Follow* was published in 1956. I read this book while growing up in the early 1980s. Like any kid, I was trying to make sense of my world. One of the selections, a Thanksgiving origin story called "Giving Is Thanks," by Amy Morris Lillie, centered on a Native American boy named Morning Bird and a white girl he had never seen before. He found her golden hair and blue eyes intriguing.

The white-blonde hair of two of my first-grade classmates fascinated me; my classmates, in turn, were drawn to my hair, which my mother plaited into two long braids every morning. My hair was long enough that I could sit on it. I allowed one friend to hold both braids and we would gallop away, two kids chasing each other, horsing around, with my hair as the reins, the other kid holding the reins. I was the horse. This scene embarrasses me a little now, although these were my friends; I can't imagine playing the other way around, and that says something.

I cannot imagine trying to publish under a name that is not mine—or changing my name when convenient to help my writing be seen. Perhaps I lack imagination. Or arrogance. Would a rose by any other name smell as sweet?

Alexie's story "What You Pawn I Will Redeem"—about history and intergenerational memory, ancestry, antistory, homelessness, despair, redemption, time—slays me. I have taught this story for years—often ending in tears when a student reads the last paragraph aloud or when I read it aloud myself. The characters are named Jackson Jackson, the pawnbroker, the grandmother, Rose of Sharon, Junior, Agnes, Irene Muse, Honey Boy, Big Boss, Mary, the bartender, Officer Williams, Mr. Grief, and three nameless Aleut cousins. Names matter.

Some of us are not able to change our names. Some of us don't want to. Some of us will have to spell out the name no matter what that name is. These things matter—language is not separate from power. All poets know this.

One of my all-time favorite poems, "The Love of Travelers," was written by Angela Jackson. The last lines have stayed with me for over twenty years: "I have died for the smallest things. / Nothing washes off." That's basically how I feel about childhood and, really, all of life—some experiences do not fade. I found Jackson's poem, originally published in *Callaloo*, because it was included in *The Pushcart Prize, XIV: Best of the Small Presses* (1989–1990). Anthologies matter—they help circulate a poem, extending the life of a poem.

I texted my brother this morning (now forty-eight and a gastroenterologist in Rhode Island). I wanted to know how old he was when he decided to change his name and why. He texted back:

> I think the summer between 3rd and 4th grade. Was tired of people mispronouncing my name, making fun of the name, and not being able to get the bicycle license plate with samir. So that was the summer of mike.

If you are going to call yourself Yi-Fen Chou, survive an American childhood with that name. Make it through a midwestern childhood. Maybe a South Asian name will help him get into Yale or keep her out of Brown (they had quotas, you know, for South Asians). Spell out the name for your health insurance company representative over the phone.

Here is a fact: if my poem were rejected forty times, I would have believed that I was not a (good) writer. Five years ago, I had a story rejected a few times. I put it aside for two years before summoning the ovaries to send it out again. My cousin, a writer, read the story and liked it; he suggested I send it to *Granta*. Although he had never said this before, I still believed he was just being nice. Who was I to submit to *Granta*? I will always regret I did not send my work right away. By the time I sent it, the editor I had been told to send to was leaving. Finally, I sent my story out once more; it found a good home at *The Literary Review*. The story, "The Half King," is about my usual obsessions: Rochester, Native Americans, ethnicity, South Asian-ness, imaginary homelands, the past, growing older, being young in New York City. Evoking a sense of place. How to make a life as an artist, what it means to live in the rust belt, in a city whose best days may be behind it.

There's a line attributed to Toronto writer Sarah Hagi I saw on Twitter some time ago that has stayed in my head: "Lord, give me the confidence of a mediocre white man." (I've also seen this variation: "DAILY PRAYER TO COMBAT IMPOSTER SYNDROME: God give me the confidence of a mediocre white dude.") Any writer needs confidence and resilience to persist in the face of inevitable rejections. A writer of color needs more. I needed more. I have persisted for many years. I believe in the written word, and I believe in my writing; still, I did not have the confidence to risk widely and repeatedly, to risk enough. I doubted whether to send this essay out, about whether to even write this essay. I did it anyway. Feel the fear and write anyway. Write in spite of it.

Lord, give me the confidence to submit *anything* forty times and then nine more! I want to believe my words are worth listening to, worth reading, worth the time and agony of writing. Any writer does. *S as in Sufficient, E as in Enormous, J as in Jealous, A as in Anyone, L as in Loophole. S as in Samir, H as in Happiness, A as in Anand, S as in Sejal.*

[2015]

Things People Said:
An Essay in Seven Steps

1. But did your husband ride in on a horse? *South Indians don't ride in on horses; that's North Indian.*

2. Was it a big Indian wedding? I mean how many people? I mean how many hundreds? You didn't wear a white dress? But was it a traditional wedding? Did you wear a midriff-baring outfit? I saw a midriff-baring outfit in that *Marigold* movie.

3. Even my shrink: Which Indian restaurant would you recommend in the area? I tell him I don't eat Indian food out. I tell him that I only eat Indian food (and we just call it food) at my parents' house. I tell him I find this question unprofessional. If he wants my recommendation, let him pay. I'm here for his recommendations—and I pay. *Do I look like a country or restaurant guide?* My husband (Indian; not that it matters) says you're just going there for a reason. Ignore everything else. I ruminate; I steam. I think about changing doctors, but there's a shortage of shrinks in our area. And he takes our insurance. The shrink tells me he has been to India, too. He can't remember the name of the city, but it's a big one.

Seven is a significant number in Hindu wedding ceremonies. Google it.

4. But how neat is that? That you and your husband are both Indian. That you were the only two Indians at your job. I mean it was fated! It's just perfect because you're both Indian. It's perfect. South Asian? I think of that as Vietnamese and Laotian. I mean, why not say Indian? Isn't that what you are? That's what I meant. Indian-American. Oh. Indian American.

5. I've never heard of it. I've been to Goa and to Bombay and somewhere else—where the Taj Mahal is. I know India has so many dialects; there are like hundreds. Tamil and Gujarati are entirely different languages? Oh, OK, Gu-ja-ra-ti. It's like different cultures? Well of course Polish and French are different languages.

6. You don't wear rings? But my daughter's Indian friend had a ring. It was a big diamond. How will people know you are married? Indian weddings: I love how colorful they are! Was it so colorful? Like a Bollywood movie? I love all those outfits. Did it take four days? My daughter went to an Indian wedding and it took four days.

7. If you have any extra invitations, I'd love to be invited. If you have any extra invitations, I'd love to see an Indian wedding. I've never been to one. I mean, they are so beautiful. I mean: I'd really like to go.

[2016]

Temporary Talismans

There's a postcard I've kept propped on my desk, on a bookshelf, or protected in a drawer since middle school. I don't know what attracted me to that particular postcard from Germany. Perhaps it was that I had not yet traveled out of the country, other than to go to Canada. But it always felt more mysterious to me than that. The image even surfaced in a story I wrote several years ago called "The Girl with Two Brothers": "We walk toward a mountain. We long for the curve in the road. We look at each other, heads leaning in. You are carrying a staff. The girl's face is happy. I could never see your face."

The postcard shows a pair of towheaded children embarking on a journey; they resemble my idea of Hansel and Gretel, though on a happier trek. I think I most likely found the card at one of those pop-up fairs of antiques, collectibles, and memorabilia that suburban malls used to host in their large corridors and courtyards. I loved looking at old bottles, books, and ephemera, and I bought this one card. It had been sent already. It was used, and it was perfect.

According to Christian McEwen in her thoughtful and timely book *World Enough and Time: On Creativity and Slowing Down*, we've lost something by losing our paper correspondence—letters and postcards. McEwen writes that "because of their brevity, and the play between words and image, postcards are perhaps especially potent."

McEwen meditates on the corporeality of the postcard—as an art object, as a temporary talisman:

> And the pleasure of a postcard in and of itself: a tiny icon which can be propped on a mantelpiece or a bedside table, attached with magnets to the fridge, slipped into the edge of a mirror, or pasted on the front of a journal, is a loss that no one even seems to mourn. And yet a postcard—just because it is so cheap, so light, so portable—can be astonishingly resilient and evocative. Who has not opened a book to find a battered postcard thrust between the pages? Who has not puzzled over a date, a smudgy postmark, and reread the message from so long ago, studying the ease or awkwardness of phrasing, the swirl of a signature . . .

I have three friendships that grew out of postcard correspondences. I met Wendy and Holly at an artist residency (fourteen and six years ago, respectively), and Michael at a conference eleven years ago. We were all already writers. But the four of us, individually, also had a practice of writing postcards to friends—and we all still do.

I have never lived in the same area as these friends, and three of us have moved in the ensuing years—between us, we've relocated in that time from or to Michigan, New York, Massachusetts, Iowa, and Washington State. When a letter or postcard arrives in the mail, I would and do recognize each of their handwriting without a signature. It gives me such pleasure to know their handwriting. In general, I don't know the handwriting of my newer friends.

Michael mentions peonies from when he lived in Syracuse. Holly writes of books and walks in her balletic, elegant script. Wendy's letters fill the page, billowing clouds—a kind of kinetic energy—I see a sail filled—telling me of the relief she feels that the school year is over. What does it mean to take the time to write a card and procure a stamp when I can message any one of them on Facebook or text or email? It's not that I do not email or message or text them now; I have and I do. But we still write postcards.

Postcards lend themselves in a quiet way to cultivating a new friendship or courting a new friend, which perhaps is why we began that way. But why do we continue? It's a quality of mind I'm after or trying to describe. A postcard arises from a quiet place, before picking up the pen—I think it's about attention and intention, although there can also be something breezy or even rushed, offhand about a postcard, at least in the time before email. Now, a postcard reads more deliberately than an email.

Postcards are incomplete, imperfect, and often say something about one's travel or daily life—they free us from the sense of having to write something extraordinary or profound. They are a first and only draft. For me, as a writer, that's such a relief. It's a snapshot of a life.

I often edit emails, but in postcards, it's okay to be free-ranging, to not get everything—or even anything—special in. All is forgiven and the stakes are low. The gesture itself takes some effort and care. It's an unexpected bit of happiness in the mail. Sometimes a flash of watercolor or a small quote, writing what we were doing and thinking, an acknowledgement of the card just received. A picture for no reason. An email wants something from you—an answer, some information, a reply. A postcard asks for nothing. It is a gift.

I became friends with Wendy, Michael, and Holly in part through years of writing. Certainly we had a connection when we met and conversations that sparked and felt meaningful. And yet, there was something about the years of trading small messages, the effort taken in going to the post office, in picking a card, in retrieving the address. The old-fashioned practice of having a pen pal, of maintaining a correspondence, tending to a conversation that became, over the years, friendship.

The postcard I've kept for so many years: it's not currently in rotation on my desk, but I safeguard it in a box with a few other talismans, art objects, muse-callers. There's a phrase in German on the picture side of the card. *Hinaus in die Ferne*! According to Google Translate, it means "Out into the Distance." In all those years, I had never bothered to look it up. I didn't need to. The image had its own potency—it gave me words. It spoke to me as if from a dream, and I trusted it fully. To step onto the path with a sense of wonder— whether setting off to write something or on an actual journey, a pilgrimage.

The card said nothing extraordinary—or perhaps what it said was essential, only words, a message (which would now come by email or text or WhatsApp). No punctuation, a sort-of poem: "We arrived / here today / Everything is / great / Valney & Esther."

♥

This week, while out of town, I went to IKEA. After I gave up sticking to my list, I left the Swedish behemoth with, among other things, a pack of postcards. The illustrations are of single birds (though no blue jays)—and therefore, have nothing to do with Toronto, where I bought them. Still, I fancied the pale green background and the image of a solitary bird perched on each card. I will send them to Michael, Wendy, and Holly when I get home.

[2016]

Six Hours from Anywhere
You Want to Be

Rochester, Syracuse, Buffalo, and the Southern Tier all hang onto the moniker "Northeast" by their fingernails. In a short story I wrote a few years ago, I describe western New York as "disturbingly close to Ohio." New York is part of both the Northeast and the Mid-Atlantic states. I thought I grew up on the East Coast. It wasn't until I left for college that I realized my mistake. (New England lets you know *they* are the oldest, *they* are the coast, *they* are the Cape.) New York: we are the only state whose borders touch both a Great Lake and the Atlantic Ocean.

I harbored this irrational aversion to Ohio—it's one reason I never considered Oberlin College, and I think it could have been a good fit for me. Somehow, I had absorbed that you were supposed to either go east, as my father and brother had for school, or west to California, where nearly all of my extended family lives. Ohio seemed lame—even more so than Rochester. I was afraid of being midwestern. Rochester: we weren't New York City, but at least we shared a state.

If you travel abroad, people will ask you where you live, and you will inevitably hear about how amazing New York City is. You can either nod your head in agreement or explain that you live over five hours away from that New York. And that where you live is nothing like it.

♥

In 2004, I moved to the Midwest for a visiting assistant professorship at a small Lutheran college. Decorah is a town of eight thousand nestled in the limestone bluffs of northeast Iowa. Decorah, home to Vesterheim, the National Norwegian-American Museum and Heritage Center, and to the annual Nordic Fest, is two and a half hours from Iowa City; it's closer to Rochester, Minnesota, than to the famed Writers' Workshop.

I remember trying to find a brunch place open on a Sunday. I found *one*. Brunch wasn't part of the larger culture there. Most everyone went to some sort of church service. No bookstore or coffee shop stayed open much past five or was open at all on a Sunday.

My friend Sarah said, "You have to have people over." (Sarah— Michigan native, close friend from college—had lived all over the country and in Brazil and Nigeria, and then returned to the Midwest to teach at the University of Iowa.)

"I'm the new one there," I complained.

"People can be reserved. And also," she said (knowing my fear of cooking), "if you have a potluck, you're going to get a lot of hot dish. That is what we call casserole. And three-bean salad. You'll get that, too."

I don't actually remember what people brought, but it was a good night. Once I acclimated to the pace and weather and made friends, I fell in love with Decorah and the Upper Midwest. I've been back to the area to visit six times since I left.

♥

Rochester sits a few miles from Lake Ontario and belongs to the Great Lakes ecosystem, which spans several states. During the six years I lived in New York City, I belonged to a writing group: Melissa grew up in Buffalo close to Lake Erie; Nora grew up in London, Ontario, and then lived in Toronto, which is right by Lake Ontario; Mike grew up in Indiana, eight miles from Lake Michigan; and I grew up nine miles from Lake Ontario, though we rarely went to the lake (those were years of zebra mussels, algae blooms, and closed beaches). We called ourselves the Great Lakes Writing Group. We have different sensibilities as writers, but we shared a sense of being outsiders in a particular way. Melissa said it best: she sometimes still can't believe she got out of Buffalo—and that the fear of someday having to move back still lingers. For me, the fear was about staying—of somehow having not gotten out of your way in order to become who you are. I had to leave Rochester. It was never even a choice.

I escaped—for eighteen years—and then I moved back. My job ended, the cost of living was low, and I knew I could stay with my family for a while. My friend Brandon used to say, "Rochester: six hours from anywhere you want to be." And we would laugh and laugh. Back then, we lived in Rochester.

Then I thought about it and worried that it was true. Brandon lives in London now. Where did I want to be?

In her novel *Jasmine*, Bharati Mukherjee wrote, "The world is divided between those who stay and those who leave." I first read those words over twenty years ago. Even then, I wanted to be someone who left. I did leave home and kept moving. I left, but more fundamentally I am someone who stays. I am someone who returns.

These days, I wonder who I am in this landscape, traveling streets on which I have driven or been driven, on which I have walked or biked or run, since my earliest memories. East, Highland, University, Clover, Elmwood, Winton, Monroe. My mother, father, and brother all left the countries of their birth to live their adult lives elsewhere. It feels strange to have returned to my hometown instead of venturing even farther out.

And then I remember Wendell Berry and his poem "Stay Home." Berry left New York City to return to his native Kentucky, where he lives on a farm, and has devoted himself to writing about the land, localism, environmental issues:

> I will wait here in the fields
> to see how well the rain
> brings on the grass.
> In the labor of the fields
> longer than a man's life
> I am at home. Don't come with me.
> You stay home too.

I will be standing in the woods
where the old trees
move only with the wind
and then with gravity.
In the stillness of the trees
I am at home. Don't come with me.
You stay home too.

Last December, R and I, recently married, needed to return some registry items to Crate and Barrel. (It turns out no one needs that many glasses.) The closest store is in Toronto, three hours away; however, you can't return items purchased in the United States to a store in another country. So we had to drive farther and in a different direction to reach the next-closest store. It was neither downstate nor in New Jersey. We drove four hours, crossing state lines to go to Cleveland. Everyone I tell this story to thinks it sounds crazy.

I was from Ohio and didn't even know it. R's favorite school is The Ohio State University. I find the "The" in the official name ridiculous. When we were dating, he told me about the NBA player LeBron James. James was on the news in 2014 for something or other; I shrugged and said, "Why would I care?" I don't follow sports. It was a big deal in part because James left Miami to return to Ohio—he returned to his home state to once again play for the Cleveland Cavaliers. He came home. I said, "Oh—so I'm like the LeBron James of Rochester!" We had a good laugh.

♥

Before we left Cleveland, we stopped at Dick's Sporting Goods, a store I had never been to. R wanted me to pick out an Ohio State University T-shirt. My brother-in-law graduated from Ohio State, and my husband has followed OSU sports ever since his brother was a student there. I went to one of those public high schools that prides itself on sending students to name-brand schools: the Ivies, Seven Sisters, Michigan, Oberlin, Wesleyan, Berkeley. I graduated from a women's college, and the only games I've ever been to and cheered for are Division III women's basketball. I have a complete disdain for and utter lack of interest in big-money men's sports. If someone had told me in high school I would not only buy but also wear a Big 10 T-shirt, I would never have believed them.

♥

We had such a nice time in Cleveland that we talked about going back. An easy drive, a waterfront to explore, good restaurants. Another Great Lakes city. I think we'll return, but still—often we just want to be at home. We could drive four hours—or we could just stay home.

[2016]

No One Is Ordinary;
Everyone Is Ordinary

Whenever my brother and I have talked about depression or therapy, which have both been part of my life for over half of it, he will bring up the film *Ordinary People*. Before I'd seen it, I wondered why he always mentioned a movie from the eighties. I knew the basic storyline: it was about a boy whose brother had died. My brother saw it for a class in high school. I watched the film for the first time a few weeks ago.

I texted him: "Was it Mrs. Lipson for Psych?"

"Critical Thinking and Writing," my brother texted back. "Mr. Musgrave. He left. He was awesome."

I knew Judith Guest, who had written the best-selling novel on which the film was based, only because she had also written the foreword to Natalie Goldberg's classic book about making a writing life, *Writing Down the Bones*. I wanted to see *Ordinary People* because I was spending a few weeks in Lake Forest—the luxe, picture-perfect suburb of Chicago where the movie was filmed.

At my suggestion, some of the others at Ragdale, a working retreat for writers and artists, and I watched the film together on an old-school TV (pre–flat screen) in a comfortable, dimly lit living room. Watching the film with people I had just met was an unusual experience—one that I found oddly moving. We sat and talked over wine—a screenwriter, a few novelists, an essayist, a poet, and a painter—about the setting, characterization, plot, pacing, and deliberate, effective use of music. We even talked about our own siblings.

I would not have watched *Ordinary People* at home with my husband because it is about the trauma a family endures after the sudden death of a son and beloved older brother—a trauma that my husband's family experienced years before I met them.

To watch the film was occasionally uncomfortable. The camera shots are long. There are pauses. Timothy Hutton's pained looks, Mary Tyler Moore's tightness and control in gesture and facial expressions, Donald Sutherland's genial helplessness. I did love seeing the world of 1980 again on the small screen: the preppy Fair Isle crewneck sweaters sported by Elizabeth McGovern and the other high school girls.

It had been years since I had watched a movie with friends on a couch in a living room. *Ordinary People* gripped me— Mary Tyler Moore's WASP coldness, her inability to connect to her surviving son; the son's stint in a psychiatric hospital and his attempts to articulate his pain. Everyone stumbling around what can't be said. Timothy Hutton as Conrad Jarrett shivering in swim practice, folding his arms across his thin chest; Mary Tyler Moore straightening something on a table so that it is just so; Donald Sutherland running and then stumbling along the shore of Lake Michigan. Judd Hirsch as the Jewish psychiatrist Conrad sees—who is kind, who is tough, who helps Conrad to connect.

"Why," I asked my brother, "did you like the film so much?"

"So many messages. Look at the title. Everyone has problems underneath. Just because you are smart doesn't mean you can work everything out yourself."

Both my brother-in-law and Conrad's brother in the film died suddenly. The visual that struck me the most in *Ordinary People* was the kitchen table, shown repeatedly. At one time, it would have been set for four, but now it had three place settings. The way a family must rearrange itself from a rectangle or square or circle into a triangle, into an ellipse, something oblong, something lopsided. Symmetry and shape broken, and so altered.

After we watched the film that night, I mentioned my brother and his love of the movie. I mentioned my brother-in-law, that it was now seventeen years since he passed. A woman I had spoken to only briefly before, sitting on the couch next to me, told us that her sister was in a psychiatric hospital. She and I stayed in the living room talking until late, after everyone else had left. We still stay in touch now.

Two of my graduate school fiction professors at UMass Amherst wrote books about their siblings and their relationships with them. In *Brothers and Keepers*, John Edgar Wideman wrote about his younger brother, who had been sentenced to prison for life without parole. Jay Neugeboren also wrote about his younger brother, who had been in and out of mental institutions and hospitals for most of his life, in his memoir *Imagining Robert*. Neugeboren once said that your sibling relationships are often your longest primary relationship.

My graduate school years in Massachusetts seemed at the time like an extension of high school or college. (I was not alone in thinking this; several of my classmates not only sensed this about our program but celebrated it—they threw an MFA prom every spring.) Western Massachusetts, also called the Pioneer Valley, had the nickname the Happy Valley. Everyone was aspiring, educated, liberal, and under forty. We were always at bars or in bookstores, in class or at readings, at concerts or in coffee shops. We had time. I had time, but the most severe depression of my life flattened me in that most picturesque valley.

A few years later, LeeAnne, my closest friend from UMass, took her life at thirty-six. She had been depressed. She had been an older sister to me. Two other friends from UMass have died in the past few years, at forty and forty-two, both in wrenching circumstances. Last year I married my husband, who lost his only brother when they were both still in their twenties. None of this is extraordinary; everyone loses someone—everyone will.

To say their names—this is one way to keep the people you love alive:

LeeAnne Smith White. The eldest of seven. We went to the Brimfield Antique Flea Market together and brought home too much stuff. We liked to drink vanilla au laits on Fridays after teaching our composition classes. She called my brother, worried, when I was depressed.

Mary Margaret Reda. The youngest of five. She introduced me to restorative yoga (you could exercise *and* lie down at the same time—brilliant!). Our best friends married each other in Maine. She wrote her dissertation on quiet students.

James Wright Foley. The eldest of five. He had the best laugh. We both loved Junot Díaz's book *Drown.* Jim had this restlessness and this charm; he listened hard when you talked. He became a conflict journalist, reporting on the lives of civilians. He was kidnapped and later murdered in Syria.

Mahesh Venkatesh Singaravelu. The elder of two. He was friends with everyone. He threw parties in high school when his parents went to India. We knew three people in common. I never went to those parties. We never met. This is my start.

[2016]

Ring Theory

Six months after my husband tied an ornate gold mangalsutra around my neck and friends showered us with rice, I chose a wedding ring. Under the noontime Chennai sun, the center stone glowed, a cabochon dome. Inside the store, the ring spoke quietly: reserved, a dark, almost dull magenta, set with two tiny diamonds. Yellow gold, typical Indian gold, South Indian temple-style setting. I picked this ring halfway around the world from where we live in Rochester, at a store in Chennai my parents-in-law have frequented for years. They designed my wedding necklace here and bought the other jewelry I wore, all of it presented as part of the ceremony. I had not chosen any of this adornment; it was, per tradition, my in-laws' choice.

ARCHITECTURAL

Three years earlier, I flew to New Mexico for a friend's birthday, a week after my own. We had once been roommates, long been friends. We spent one afternoon in Santa Fe, wandering the Georgia O'Keeffe Museum—the reason my friend chose New Mexico. O'Keeffe was a strong woman, an individual, an artist we both admired. In the gift shop, a particular designer's rings called to both of us—sturdy, each different, each with an architectural quality. I am usually drawn to simpler, smaller jewelry, though larger pieces look sharper and suit me. My friend and I deliberated over who would buy what, but different rings called to each of us. I found mine: thick-banded and modernist, a statement in a way I don't tend to make. They were inexpensive: we marked our fortieth birthdays with jewelry that cost less than forty dollars.

Now my New Mexico ring is discolored from wear and water. I wore it every day for the two years I taught ninth graders. I wore it during the two months my grandmother was in the hospital and in rehab for her stroke; I did not remove it when I washed my hands at school or in restaurants or at the hospital.

This ring had presence, declaring itself without shouting. It evoked the moon, the sun, an egg, a shield; a talisman in motion, a pendulum at the moment of pause.

SILVER

Later that week, my friend and I drove south, to White Sands National Monument. She had signed us up for a moonrise walk there, and we treaded and twirled, taking photos of shadows, across all that sparkling (in sun) then glowing (in dusk) sand (was it once an ocean). It was a desert: beautiful-barren—stark. The dunes recalled salt flats I had seen in Sicily, a lifetime ago in my twenties, wearing a silver ring from Mexico I've since lost. The dunes and the silver ring reminded me of all that had slipped by unnoticed, all that had happened, and had not happened, since then. What we knew or didn't know about friendship, about time; about which jewelry lasts and for how long; about which friendships last and for how long; about how meaning morphs with age; about age itself.

HAMMERED

A few years ago, I left New York City, unwilling, when it came down to it, to hustle. I had not found a partner, not secured a book contract or tenure. All the golden handcuffs. But I didn't want to stay on the treadmill or in the water, treading, waiting for life to begin. I did not want to lean in. I opted out. I landed in India, and traveled for a few months. Then I moved back home. Before all that, I threw a ring into the East River—a hammered silver one I had bought for the interview for the job I had just left. It was my longest relationship, that job. After six years, leaving was my divorce.

MANGALSUTRA

In western New York, I marry a teacher who had grown up two miles from me, just outside Rochester. We live here, ten miles from the shore of Lake Ontario, the smallest of the Great Lakes. His parents chose the mangalsutra and the particular design of the pendant. He is South Indian, I am North Indian, and we are Hindu. He is Tamilian, I am Gujarati, we are ourselves. We place flowers in water, we perform rituals at the temple, at home; we are told to gaze at the full moon, to drink in the moonlight, and there are special full-moon pujas. He is not an artist, but it is an art of sorts—marriage—learning a way to live together.

I usually vacillate, take time to decide. Yet that first ring was easy, like something out of Georgia O'Keeffe's world, harsh in its beauty and also elegant. An amulet, a protection, a shield, a decorated sword: proud, confident—not bashful. What a strong woman would wear when she's single and has just lost her job. And maybe she hasn't published her first book, but who's counting?

Is it strange to have such a strong feeling about a ring? When I decided to marry my husband, no ring leapt out and said, "Here. This. Here I am." Even after I got married. Perhaps part of it was that no engagement or wedding ring I tried on or found looked right with my New Mexico ring on.

I did not want him to choose a ring. "I'll be wearing it," I said. How could someone else choose it?

BRASS RING

During the year we were engaged, I wore a slim, inexpensive, hexagonal brass ring made by a local designer we knew, bought by my husband at a shop I liked. Though I did not choose it, I wore the ring on my left pinky, and it stamped a moss green band around the base of that finger, ghostly, oxidizing. But the whole time I was engaged, that whole year, I wore my New Mexico ring on my middle finger and an almost invisible band on my pinky finger. And no other rings. Nothing on my ring finger.

I consult the dictionary. A brass ring (informal) refers to "wealth, success, or a prestigious position considered as a goal or prize, e.g.: few of those who reach for the brass ring of the presidency achieve it."

A month before my husband presented me with the brass ring (though we had already decided to marry), my in-laws hosted a ceremony in their home, according to South Indian tradition. This event proclaimed our engagement: a document signed by our parents and my brother and sister-in-law; a priest from Toronto; a fire ceremony, chanting, lunch, many flowers; our immediate families and my grandmother, aunt, nephews, cousin, and cousin-in-law present. No rings. I wasn't even sure I wanted one.

Getting engaged and married is considered an achievement in the countries and cultures to which I belong by birth and ancestry, by nationality and ethnicity, by language and skin, by blood and memory, by gender and age. I did not want getting married to be the greatest achievement of my life.

TIFFANY RING

A month before the wedding, my sister-in-law and I ducked into Tiffany's, an unplanned side trip at the Providence Place Mall. I slipped on solitaires and halos and snapped a few photos to send my fiancé. Oddly thrilling, that sea-green, blue-green store! But eleven thousand dollars? Ridiculous, obscene, lacking imagination. Ostentatious, ethically dubious, suburban, traditional, not to mention tacky, buying into the status quo.

Engagement rings seem to be about signaling how much your fiancé is able or willing to spend. I didn't want to signal anything. My family originally hails from Gujarat, India. Gujaratis have traditionally worked in the diamond industry;

some of my relatives are still in it. Diamonds are important in our culture—a symbol of status. But I never liked diamonds; I wanted something less obvious and more artistic. But after the wedding I began to scroll through designs. My husband told me about the four C's: carat, cut, color, and clarity. I had never bothered to learn anything about diamonds. They had seemed so superficial. And later so attractive.

Months after I was married, I couldn't stop staring at women's hands at the gym, in yoga classes; at readings, at parties, at bars. Blood diamonds be damned. They sparkled. Turns out I wasn't immune to noticing that. And sparkly: I could see how the parade could topple a person.

TOTEM

I lost the card that came with my New Mexico ring but searched Google until I dredged up the name. The designer, Christophe Poly, is Montreal-based. The rings, unique and particular, require care. Wear them in water, you ruin them.

Right now, my hands are swollen, and I can wear no rings. But I could never wear both, and that has been hardest: I knew this to be true the day we bought the wedding ring, and even more when I wore it all the days that followed.

When I bought the New Mexico ring, I chose myself, my life, without needing to prove anything to anyone. I had already failed, and still, I was happy.

Nothing has felt right in terms of an engagement or wedding ring. I debated returning to my New Mexico ring: sometimes adornment can serve as both talisman and totem, speaking for who we are. Then months pass, and we can never wear a thing again, or not for a while, leaving it to lie unworn and forlorn. Yet for a time, a pendant or ring can hold such power: an emblem filled with energy, force, intention, love.

METAL

Once I married, I found it almost impossible to be the self I had previously forged. Isn't the point of an engagement ring or wedding ring that it should trump your other rings? It is the thing that shows, that is meant to be noticed. Recently, I slipped on a plain band, something cheap I found in my jewelry drawer. It suited me. My husband agreed. A nondescript metal. I didn't want the fact of my being married to be the most noticeable thing about me.

The problem is I have never been simple. Though I knew my husband was the right one, I never felt that way about a ring. Now my hands are swollen, and I wear no rings. Not swollen from pregnancy, just mysterious swelling, from punching these words, perhaps.

AMULET

In India, I found a quiet-eyed cabochon, a cipher. The Burmese ruby has no flash, no game—it is a non-neon digital crimson, polished, not cut, modest and understated. Too understated? We would leave Chennai in a few days and I was afraid if I did not choose a ring there, when I had a deadline, I might never do it.

I wear my wedding ring when I go out, and the mangalsutra to the temple and sometimes when I dress up. During the day, when writing or at the gym or preparing to teach, I wear nothing, my hands clicking away on keys, typing. No nail polish, no rings.

Two years after the wedding, I call my father-in-law to ask what the mangalsutra means, why it matters to them—to my mother-in-law, especially—that I wear it. I know it identifies me as married. But I had never seen the pendant's design before, nor would I have chosen it. "It's a representation of Ganesh," he says. The remover of obstacles. To protect one from harm. To protect one's husband from harm. Who wouldn't want that? I will wear my necklace more.

In a silver dish, the New Mexico ring and my wedding ring sit side by side. My mangalsutra lies coiled in my dresser drawer cupped in a hollowed-out gourd. I look at them; they look back at me. I wait for them to speak; I wait for the next talisman to enter my life, to be summoned, to appear—and to remind me of what I do not wish to forget.

[2017]

Saris and Sorrows

We had not wanted an elaborate wedding. We wanted our friends and family present, our communities. Our wedding was big, but not for the reasons you /Americans might assume (Bollywood spectacle, large families, over the top). Only a few relatives on my husband's side attended—most of them live in India and Malaysia and could not be present. My extended family is small and in the United States. All of them, most crucially my grandmother, attended our wedding. We married in our hometown where our parents had lived for forty years, and they had their lists of who *had* to be invited; they had attended the weddings of all of their friends' children. I had close friends in each of the places I lived—when single and moving for work, you have to make your own family.

My parents and in-laws recognized each other from the Hindu Temple but had never met. They belonged to different communities (Gujarati, Tamilian) with few overlaps in their guest lists. A Hindu wedding does not join two individuals, but instead two families, witnessed by their communities. To include both of our communities meant a small wedding was impossible.

♥

My father-in-law created a profile for his son on Tamil-matrimony.com, a marriage site made for people of Tamil origin. My in-laws worried as the years went by. R turned thirty, then thirty-five.

Father-in-law in an email to me:

> I discarded the information once he got engaged. Basically, it spelled out the bio data like date of birth, age, height, color of complexion, birth star (anusham), raisi (virchigam), educational qualifications, current career.

> Personal information: soft natured, family oriented, helpful nature and concern for the deprived, tennis player and coach. Future bride's requirements: well educated preferably with a master's degree, can peruse [pursue]* a career, family oriented, and tall. Preferably the birth stars should match.

That my in-laws don't have parents or siblings in the United States made them even more concerned. Five years ago, R and I met at work not through a matrimonial—at the school where he had taught for many years and where I was a new teacher. He saw my photo and bio before we met, in the new faculty hires email sent to everyone at our school. He told me he made a point of meeting me. R kept stopping by my classroom and suggesting that we catch up. I said sure, but thought, *How can we catch up? We don't even know each other! Maybe it's the "You're Indian, I'm Indian, let's have lunch and I'll give you the lay of the land thing."* Later I found out it was the "Are you single because I want to ask you on a date" thing. Not the Indian thing. Less than two months after our first date, we knew. I made a list of possible bridesmaids.

*I did pursue a career, but it's safe to say I also perused them.

We met with two separate wedding planners. I had never once in my life thought about colors or themes. My father-in-law made the appointments. My idea of a theme: we're getting married! The colors: bright, like any Indian wedding. Gold jewelry and many bangles—always many bangles. As we left the office of one planner, my father-in-law shook his head. "Too much money. I can do it better than that." My father-in-law had worked for Xerox in its heyday, and as one small part of his job he planned their annual holiday party for over a thousand employees. In the end, we hired no one. My father-in-law planned our wedding. He knew he would do a better job.

There is no such thing as a typical Indian wedding. Though I married another Indian, my wedding did not resemble my parents' or any of my friends' ceremonies.

When I asked him about the ceremony later, my father-in-law said, "Look at the wedding book. So much is explained." Still, he relented and answered my questions. Why were we wearing turmeric-stained yellow thread strung with a gold coin wound around our foreheads? (Gujaratis don't do that.)

Email response:

> The mother in law by tying [a] pattam to her new daughter in law gives up the management of the family, so far held by her, in favor of her daughter in law (assuming the daughter in law knows how to cook).

That's a shot at me. I email back, "Ha, ha, Dad."

My in-laws consulted astrologists: the only date in June for a wedding was one Friday at 8:30 a.m. My parents and I wanted the wedding to take place on a Saturday. A Friday morning wedding and Saturday evening reception would require multiple nights in a hotel room for our out-of-town family and friends. Gujaratis think of budgets, cost. Three nights at a hotel is not thrifty.

My father-in-law: "Hindu weddings don't take place on Saturdays."

"That isn't true," I said. "My parents married on a Saturday in India. They're Hindu. Every Hindu wedding I've attended took place on a Saturday." (Except my brother's. My sister-in-law is also South Indian, and their wedding was on a Friday.)

My father-in-law: "South Indians only get married on Fridays or Sundays. Tuesdays are possible, but not Saturdays."

"I'm not South Indian," I said. I didn't say: "I'm the bride." I thought it, though.

I didn't count. It was not my wedding.

♥

We married at the moment my husband tied the yellow thread of my mangalsutra around my neck. We didn't have rings. On the mandap, my brother, my parents, my in-laws, my sister-in-law, the priest, my husband, and I leaned in, tottered. My father almost fell off the platform—it had been built too small to hold so many people. No one's clothes caught on fire, though there had been some concern about this. Three, then four garlands of white, pink, red, and purple carnations and roses covered most of my sari. Jasmine flowers decorated the lamps for the puja. Strands of fragrant white jasmine were pinned in my hair—this is a Tamilian tradition I love.

♥

South Indians (at least Tamilians and Kannadigas) have formal engagement ceremonies. R and I say we wish our engagement ceremony had been the wedding. The ceremonies are small: just family at the house with a priest. My father-in-law had a special document printed to formalize the engagement—it lists our names, our grandparents' names, our parents' names, and the date of the wedding. In retrospect, the day felt easy. My twin nephews roll their eyes in photos, skeptical. They wear blue and white Nehru collar cotton shirts I bought them in Delhi. They are growing fast, wrists sticking out from their sleeves. We framed a photo of R and me with our parents, the six of us beaming and relieved.

We didn't know how complicated things would get. We didn't know about my grandmother's stroke, still six months away; about my aunt's cancer recurrence or that she would leave Chicago and move in with my parents, grandmother, and me that fall for her treatment. So much sickness and sadness.

♥

It always seemed to me that weddings had more to do with the bride's side of the family. Not my wedding.

Why must a Gujarati have a Tamilian ceremony? I didn't want to. I'm not South Indian. I like South Indian food and dance, I studied Bharata Natyam and Kuchipudi, but I am Gujarati.

Who makes these rules?

Gujarati wedding sari colors: red and white, sometimes with an accent color of green. I didn't know about the green until I went shopping—all the ones I'd seen were red and white. As was my mom's.

Tamilians don't wear white at weddings (only at funerals). In a South Indian Tamilian Hindu ceremony, the bride leaves halfway through, exits the stage to change from her sari into one chosen by her in-laws, and then returns in the second sari, to symbolize her joining the husband's family. I would not have agreed to do this, had I known the symbolism. I already had a family—now I would have two. I had no plans to take leave of mine.

My aunt: "A lot of girls these days just wear gagra cholis or lehengas."

My father-in-law: "In a Hindu wedding, you have to wear a sari."

Gujarati brides wear one sari. Then something different for the reception—chuniya chori—easier to dance in them. These are made for Navaratri, garba, raas, dancing. I have never loved dressing up. Hindu ceremonies and Gujarati anythings involve heavy saris (literally heavy—embroidered with sequins, gold thread, mirrorwork, beading, borders). You have to suck in your stomach, pull the drawstrings of the petticoat tight around your waist so when part of the six yards is tucked into it, the petticoat doesn't sag or fall off.

I said, "I don't want to change saris halfway through the ceremony. I don't want to take out a thousand safety pins and change jewelry halfway through. Also, it's not my tradition." We fought over this up until the week before the wedding. I asked later what if I hadn't changed.

My father-in-law laughed. "But you did."

Both my brother's wife, South Indian and Bangalore-born, and a college friend of mine from Madras explained that it didn't count as a wedding if you didn't change saris. Didn't count to whom? Who counted here? What about the one wearing the sari?

At the end of it all, I liked the sari my in-laws picked out in Chennai better than the one I bought. In my favorite wedding photo (the only one we framed), I wear the flame-colored silk Kanchipuram sari threaded with a design of gold lotus blossoms. R wears a jubba, a long shirt, salmon-colored, and a white veshti, a pure silk sarong worn by South Indian men. A few years after the wedding, when we looked at all the photos again, my father-in-law said, "The sari we picked out for you suited you better than the one you picked." This annoyed me, but he was right.

I liked my Gujarati sari, the cream-colored panethar with the red-and-green border. I liked the red silk Kanchipuram sari better. My in-laws spent months shopping while in Chennai for the winter; I spent two bitter days in February in Toronto (not recommended), the closest place to shop for wedding clothes. My friend P flew from Brooklyn to Rochester to help, and R drove us to Toronto. We could not use our phones—I had not remembered to research Canadian rates and plans—so navigating an unfamiliar, frozen city, finding store hours and directions, added an extra level of stress given how much we had come to rely on internet access.

I hated the pressures and details of wedding planning, the long lists of to-dos for things I had never thought of. That was my life, then. I taught *Romeo and Juliet* to four classes of ninth graders and helped take care of my grandmother who had gone from making dinner every night to needing help to eat and to walk. She struggled to speak. My mother and aunt shouldered the round-the-clock heavy labor of caregiving, and visiting family and I took shifts, everyone stretched, exhausted.

♥

For the wedding program, my father-in-law commissioned an artist in India to draw each step of the ceremony, to explain what each ritual meant (walking around the fire, garlands, etc.). We saw the programs a week before the wedding, but my mind wasn't on them—my half-stitched sari blouses occupied me the most—they didn't fit, and this was an event where people would notice, and there would be photos. If something looked terrible, I would see it again. In all those other weddings, I had been a bridesmaid or a guest.

The detailed program booklet highlighted some of the patriarchal aspects of Hindu ceremonies. (The "wedding sari" referred to only my second sari, the one from my in-laws.) The program cover listed four numbers: "1 auspecious* moment; 2 loving hearts; 3 solemnizing knots of the sacrament; 7 steps and vows of togetherness." While reading through the booklet we remarked that the figures in the program resembled us. Then we realized the figures *were* us: the artist had based his drawings on photos of us from our engagement ceremony. My father-in-law had seen to so many details such as this that would never have occurred to us.

Auspicious was misspelled, but everything went well. I would have caught that mistake had I seen the program beforehand, but I also would have been unhappy with some of the traditional aspects and explanations of the ceremony. So better it went the way that it went.

My father-in-law recreated a typical South Indian temple from Tamil Nadu. It stood twenty-five feet tall, trapezoidal in shape, bluish in color. In front of the temple, two tables held statues of Ganesh and Krishna. He had the hall of the convention center decorated with elephant tusks (not real), cloth columns, thoranam ("I don't know the English name," my father-in-law said; I learn it's braided fronds from the banana plant). Four musicians—two played the nadaswarm (long wind instrument) and two played a drum you hit on both sides (thavil is the Tamil name; it sounds a sharp staccato).

This, along with his whole vision of the wedding, made it into the most beautiful wedding I have ever seen or attended. I tell this to my father-in-law. He laughs and says, "You didn't attend it. You were in it. It was your wedding." The Gujarati weddings I'd been to had been lovely, but pretty interchangeable in design. My father-in-law focused on making something unique. He was especially focused because of his other son.

♥

My in-laws threw the only wedding they would ever throw. It had to be everything. Our wedding was as much or more for their older son, the one they had never written a matrimonial for. (Maybe they had? I don't know; it's not anything I could ever ask.) He was friends with everyone. No one said it, but I know—he wouldn't have needed a matrimonial. He was outgoing; people were drawn to him. I never met him, but he lives near the center of my life now.

My wedding was not about saris but about sorrows. Saris were easier to fight over than to address what was hardest: the absence of their elder son. My wedding was about R's brother.

One December night they were home. R was downstairs watching a movie, heard a noise. He went upstairs and found his brother unconscious, blood; he called 911. R rode with him in the ambulance; neighbors drove my mother-in-law. My father-in-law was in India. It was December 21, close to Christmas; all flights booked. It took him a week to get home. In 1999, R was twenty-two. My brother-in-law was only twenty-seven. He suffered a heart arrhythmia then lapsed into a coma. He never woke up.

♥

When we look at our wedding photos in their official books—two and a half years after our wedding—we see that we have no photos of our family all together. R isn't in the series of photos taken before the reception with both sides of my family and all my cousins. He and his parents are in none of them. His parents were with their guru, who had traveled here from India. R was with them first, and then gathered his shoes, suit, and tie to go over to the hotel to get dressed. He had new cufflinks, decorated with small purple flowers. They are hard to fasten by yourself.

We didn't have attendants, because it's not traditionally part of a Hindu wedding. Also, R could not imagine having groomsmen, which would only highlight that absence at the center of our wedding. If R could not have his best man, he wouldn't have anyone. The core of what this meant: R was getting dressed for his wedding by himself.

A photo taken at the end of the night, after the reception, shows my college friends with their spouses and me. We are in our hotel suite, sitting on couches or standing in front of the window. The city's modest skyline glitters behind us.

R isn't there. He is downstairs with his dad settling a bill for the DJ. It is the sort of task an older brother would have taken care of. I know this because I have that kind of older brother, too.

♥

In his speech, my father-in-law said (and didn't remember saying) that he knew R missed his brother but that I would replace him. At that terrible sweetheart table on the stage, with the two of us on display like our rose-colored cake, R burst into tears. I said I could never replace his brother. A sweetheart table is a table only for two (sort of incongruous at an Indian wedding), but a family table would only underscore who was missing. His parents had tried so hard—not to replace their older son but to find a companion for their younger son—to make sure he would not be alone when his parents were gone.

My sister-in-law and R explained what I had not understood—my in-laws were doing everything according to custom, religion, astrology, and superstition so as to set their remaining son off on a good foot and to keep him, to keep us, from harm. My brother-in-law had been rushed to the hospital with no prior warning of illness. It's something I can't quite imagine. But six months before the wedding, when my grandmother had stayed in my room because her new bed would not arrive until the next day, she had a stroke. I had turned on the light at midnight and seen her eyes widen, her mouth open, and no words coming. "Ba?" I said. No words. I dialed 911 and then my fiancé. I called him because he knew.

♥

Life is not about weddings but about cooking and dishes, laundry and work, writing, parents, teaching, taking out the recycling. I know this now. House hunting, moving, drafting a will, taxes. Making the appointment for snow tires. Determining the compromise temperature, the maximum number of blankets and books the other person can tolerate on the bed. Life is not about colors and themes or even saris. I know this now, but still, weddings astonish me: the threshold, the intention, the cusp; the crucible, the gathering, the hope.

[2019]

Voice Texting with My Mother

It has been nearly four years since our wedding. My grandmother's passing—Ba—a sharp rending in my life; my cousin's new daughter, a new life. We bought a house and are talking about curtains. After weddings are conversations with our parents, are still our conversations with each other.

I was voice texting with my mother:

> Do you have Old
> sorrows I can use as
> curtains for a while in
> my bedroom

> Or in other places
> until we get curtains?
> If so can you put
> some aside and I can
> look at them when I
> come over? Thank
> you

She texts back:

> "U mean saries?"

My hands flew, typing, my third language, now voice texting. Mothers read daughters. I posted a screenshot on Instagram. One friend writes, "I want someone to use my old sorrows as curtains in a bedroom." Another posts, "You can have my old sorrows!" I am pleased they write to me. "I have enough of my own sorrows," I tell them.

Saris and sorrows and weddings are one. These are stories to myself and to you (reader, writer, mother, mother tongue).

These are letters to myself, and to my mother; words to my grandmother, who taught me to dance.

These are stories we tell ourselves, stories we tell each other; weddings are stories we tell ourselves; we are stories we tell each other.

By *wedding*, I mean an occasion to dance. By *occasion to dance*, I mean joy. I mean to move.

Here is my booth at the carnival: What will stay, and what will go; Indian, American, and girl. The body; bones, raced, erased.

Stories are an argument between some words.

Weddings are a series of stories, a circle of stories, are bodies, streets, intersections.

We wear our sorrows, they wear us, they wind themselves around us.

This conversation still bears repeating: a circle of words is my companion, a circle of words with R, a circle of words with myself.

Words are surfacing; this is one way to dance.

Words are rising: this is how to dance.

[2002, 2019]

Acknowledgments

Thank you to the following publications in which these essays first appeared, sometimes in earlier forms:

"Skin" first appeared in *Hanging Loose* 82 (2003); republished online in *Route Nine* (2014);

"Who's Indian?" (originally titled "Where Are You From?") first appeared in *Catamaran: South Asian American Writing* 1 (2003);

"Married" first appeared in *Waxwing Literary Journal* 9 (summer 2016);

"Betsy, Tacy, Sejal, Tib" first appeared in *Under Her Skin: How Girls Experience Race in America,* edited by Pooja Makhijani (Seattle: Seal Press, 2004);

"The World Is Full of Paper. Write to Me." first appeared in *The Margins,* December 8, 2013; it was reprinted in *Mad Heart Be Brave: Essays on the Poetry of Agha Shahid Ali,* edited by Kazim Ali (Ann Arbor: University of Michigan Press, 2017);

"Kinship, Cousins, & Khichidi" first appeared in the *Massachusetts Review: Food Matters* 45, no. 3 (autumn 2004);

"Street Scene" first appeared in the *Kenyon Review Online* (fall 2011);

"Bird" first appeared in the *Kenyon Review Online* (fall 2010);

"Walking Tributaries" first appeared in *Wellesley,* the alumnae magazine of Wellesley College (fall 2011);

"Castle, Fort, Lookout, House" first appeared in the *Asian American Literary Review* (portraiture issue) 3 (fall/winter 2012);

"Curriculum" first appeared in *Conjunctions Online*, February 26, 2013;

"Your Wilderness Is Not Permanent" first appeared in *Conjunctions 72: Nocturnals* (spring 2019);

"Thank You" first appeared in *Brevity* 44 (fall 2013);

"365 Pelham Road" first appeared in *The Big Brick Review* 1 (2014);

"There Is No Mike Here" first appeared in *The Margins*, September 15, 2015, as part of "After Yi-Fen Chou: A Forum";

"Things People Said: An Essay in Seven Steps" first appeared in *Brevity* 53 (fall 2016);

"Temporary Talismans," "Six Hours from Anywhere You Want to Be," and "No One Is Ordinary; Everyone Is Ordinary" first appeared in the *Kenyon Review Blog* (on July 12, 2016; June 13, 2016; and April 1, 2016, respectively);

"Ring Theory" first appeared in *Strange Attractors: Lives Changed by Chance*, edited by Edie Meidav and Emmalie Dropkin (Amherst: University of Massachusetts Press, 2019); reprinted in *Literary Hub* (2019).

Many people and experiences contributed to this book, and there is no way to name them all. I wrote these essays over the course of twenty years; any list I make will be partial.

I had the good fortune to work closely with thoughtful editors on several of the essays. Thank you to editors Sarah Einstein and Dinty W. Moore, as well as guest editors Joy Castro and Ira Sukrungruang, of *Brevity: A Journal of Concise Literary Nonfiction*, for selecting "Things People Said: An Essay in Seven Steps" for the fall 2016 special issue of *Brevity* on Race, Racism, and Racialization; in part, that publication led to this book.

I also thank Kazim Ali (*Mad Heart Be Brave: Essays on the Poetry of Agha Shahid Ali*), Lawrence-Minh Bùi Davis (*Asian American Literary Review*), Jonny Diamond (*Literary Hub*), Gregory Gerard (*Big Brick Review*), Alice M. Hummer (*Wellesley*), Pooja Makhijani

(*Under Her Skin: How Girls Experience Race in America*, Seal Press), Anita Mannur (*Massachusetts Review*), Edie Meidav and Emmalie Dropkin (*Strange Attractors*, University of Massachusetts Press), Bradford Morrow (*Conjunctions*), Jyothi Natarajan (*The Margins*), Mark Pawlak (*Hanging Loose*), Rajini Srikanth (*Catamaran: South Asian American Writing*), and Erin Stalcup (*Waxwing*). I owe the greatest debt to Sergei Lobanov-Rostovsky at the *Kenyon Review*. To have an editor who understands something of how you think is a gift. To have an editor who becomes a mentor and friend, even more so.

At the University of Georgia Press, I wish to thank Lisa Bayer, Jason Bennett, Walter Biggins, Valerie Boyd, John Griswold, Kerrie Maynes, Erin Kirk New, Thomas Roche, Bethany Snead, Jordan Stepp, and Steven Wallace. I am especially grateful to Valerie Boyd, coeditor of Crux: The Georgia Series in Literary Nonfiction, who read my essay "Things People Said," and who reached out to invite me to submit my manuscript, and to executive editor Walter Biggins for shepherding this book through the editorial process. Thank you as well to the anonymous reviewers for their rigorous and thoughtful reading of my manuscript. I know this is a better book for their comments and suggestions.

I wish to thank my teachers, past and present. In particular, I have been thinking of my earliest teachers and professors whose classes gave me a wider context within which to see my own writing. Thank you to John Bird, aka Mr. Bird. I am grateful to Frank Bidart, Kathleen Brogan, Elena Tajima Creef, Laura Levine, Susan Reverby, and the late Claire Zimmerman, who were my professors at Wellesley College. I also thank my modern dance and choreography teacher at Wellesley, the late Dorothy Hershkowitz, and my Bharata Natyam and Kuchipudi teacher, Rathna Kumar of Houston, Texas.

A shout-out to my far-flung writing partners: Wendy Call (Seattle), Magdalena Maczynska (Brooklyn and Berlin), Holly

Wren Spaulding (Maine), and I thank Wendy for serving as a consulting editor on this manuscript and for all her counsel and practical advice. Magda, thank you for remote co-working and check-ins. I felt as though you were just across the hall in the other office, as we were for years. Holly, I'm grateful for your attention and perspective on the big picture and small details. Thank you all for making the path less lonely. I deeply appreciate our friendships and co-working writing retreats.

I wish to thank the following residencies, individuals, and fellowships and their transformative support: Blue Mountain Center, Harriet Barlow, and Ben Strader for my first artist residency in 2001 and for alumni mini residencies in subsequent years. The writers and artists I've met through Blue have shaped my life and my art practice. I thank the Consortium for Faculty Diversity (CFD) for two one-year fellowships and visiting positions at Mount Holyoke College (Massachusetts) and Luther College (Iowa). I am grateful to Marymount Manhattan College for a year-long sabbatical leave, during which I began a few of these essays.

Thanks to the Anderson Center for Interdisciplinary Studies at Tower View in Red Wing, Minnesota for a residency during which I worked on some of these words and to the Millay Colony for the Arts for a residency, off-season time and space, and workshops with Melissa Febos and Carole Maso. I am grateful to the Ragdale Foundation for two residencies, including a Ragdale Fellowship. I also wish to thank the Saltonstall Foundation for the Arts and Lesley Williamson for two brief retreats, which helped me revise and reorder these essays into a book, and the Virginia Center for the Creative Arts for their generous George Edwards and Rachel Hadas Fellowship. And to Ilse Ackerman and her family for hosting me at the Spring House while I reviewed copyedits.

I am grateful to the editors of the *Kenyon Review*—especially to Geeta Kothari, Sergei Lobanov-Rostovsky, David H. Lynn, Kirsten

Reach, and Nancy Zafris. Thank you, Geeta, for suggesting I come to Kenyon in the first place and for years of friendship.

Thank you to Kundiman, which has been a family and a literary home and heart for me—the antidote to my experiences in academia. My deepest thanks to Cathy Linh Che, Sarah Gambito, and Joseph O. Legaspi. Sarah and Joseph, thank you for creating Kundiman and making the world our younger selves needed. I am grateful to belong to a community that supports and celebrates Asian American writing. I also thank writers Rachel McKibbens and Jacob Rakovan for hosting the Western New York Kundiman Reading at their bar in Rochester, The Spirit Room, in 2018.

I grew up seeing and later studying with Garth Fagan Dance, my hometown dance company. Fagan built his internationally known company, composed almost entirely of dancers of color, in Rochester. His strong aesthetic, choreography, a movement vocabulary drawing from Afro-Caribbean and American modern dance, and wide range of artistic and musical influences impressed me. You didn't have to fit yourself into someone else's forms. Thank you, Garth, for bringing the world to Rochester, to Norwood Pennewell Jr. for years of friendship, and to Natalie Rogers-Cropper for the gift of your time and wisdom. I thank my beautiful Fagan dance teacher, Christopher Morrison, in memory.

From my time in Western Massachusetts: I wish to thank my friends, former classmates, and former professors in the English Department, MFA Program, and other departments at the University of Massachusetts at Amherst—including Chris Carrier, Margo Culley, Stephanie Dunson, Caitlin Echasseriau, Peter Elbow, James (Jim) W. Foley, Nina Ha, Noy Holland, Dale Hudson, Jay Neugeboren, Mary Reda, Josna Rege, Greg Tulonen, Andrew Varnon, Erin White, LeeAnne Smith White and Philip W. White, and Leni Zumas. Thank you also to Kum-Kum Bhavnani and Liz Hanssen at *Meridians: feminism, race, transnationalism* at Smith College, and to Floyd Cheung (also at Smith College), Jennifer Ho (Mount Holyoke College), and the Asian American Studies and American Studies community in the Five Colleges. I am grateful to Daphne Lowell and Rebecca Nordstrom at Hampshire College for their contemplative and modern dance classes and to Marilyn Hart at UMass Amherst, my first yoga teacher. At Mount Holyoke College, where I taught for a year, I thank Nilanjana Bhattacharjya, Calvin Chen, and Becky Wai-Ling Packard. Thank you to my former neighbor in Amherst, Matthew King, for attending my reading at Smith College in 2012, for insisting I needed a website, and for setting it up and helping me maintain it.

From the years I lived in New York City: I wish to thank my former colleagues at Marymount Manhattan College, especially Michael Backus, Jennifer Brown, Giovanna Chesler, Cecilia Feilla, Kathleen LeBesco, Alessandra Leri, Magdalena Maczynska, and Martha Sledge. My cousin, Suketu Mehta, for years of dinners, drinks, advice, and conversations. My Great Lakes Writing Group: Mike Backus, Nora Maynard, and Melissa Sandor. In Brooklyn, Purvi Shah, my fellow artist and former roommate. In New Jersey, my cousin Monica Shah, fellow teacher and creative. Thank you to Denise Iris for art rituals and dance classes and to Preston Merchant for many author photos and friendship over the years.

In Rochester, our excellent local writing community. I am especially grateful to Jess Fenn and Nadia Ghent for reading whole drafts of this manuscript and for their detailed comments and to Jess, Kyle Semmel, and Stephen West for feedback and our writing group. I thank Kristen Gentry, Rachel Hall, Gail Hosking, Sonja Livingston, Ravi Mangla, and Sally Parker for years of co-working companionship and friendship. Thank you to Mary Jane (MJ) Curry and Jayne Lammers for including me in the Warner School Writing Boot Camps at the University of Rochester and Fridays at Boulder. Thank you also to Albert Abonado, Peter

Conners, Robin Flanigan, Irene Galvin, Rachel McKibbens, Jacob Rakovan, Stephen Schottenfeld, Joanna Scott, Scott Seifritz, and Angelique Stevens. To Writers & Books and its dedicated staff for creating a community-based space for telling stories, reading, and writing, and for the opportunity to teach. I gratefully acknowledge my long-time students: Sally Bittner Bonn, Julie Cicora, Nadia Ghent, Donna Jackel, Kristin Kelly, and Pete Strub. It has been a pleasure to learn alongside you.

In Rochester, our local Gujarati family friends and community. To Marjana Ababovic, for being at every local reading I can remember during the last seven years, your support and presence there, and honest feedback after. For writing and yoga and adventures. You made returning to Rochester something to look forward to and also enjoy. To our neighbors, Maggie, Colin, and especially Alice ("I'm gonna lock you out") Doody. A thousand thanks to Lorraine Bohonos, Arlene Dalton, Beverly Gold. I thank Jennifer Leonard, Kate Polozie, Margie Searl, and Kitty Wise, longtime and loyal friends.

To friends who live all over: some of you are mentioned by name in this book, but all of you are in these words. Sarah Adams, Brandon Block, Brian Caton and Sandhya Purohit Caton, Natasha Chang, Neelu Chawla, Karina Corrigan, Ann Gagliardi, Jeanie Gayeski, Monica Gebell, Emily Heaphy, Brian Hessel, Uttara Bharath Kumar, Lei Ouyang, Annapurna Poduri, Kristie Shah, Elliot Shapiro, Dena B. Vardaxis, and Cat Willis. To Pat Dougherty, in memory.

To my fellow writers and artists from all over I thank you for comradeship, commiseration, and inspiration across screens and in person—including Willa Carroll, Erica Cavanaugh, Alexander Chee, Chen Chen, Kiran Desai, Parijat Desai, Aditi Dhruv, Anjali Enjeti, Sugi Ganeshananthan, Cathy Park Hong, Mira Jacob, Elizabeth Kadetsky, Madhu H. Kaza, Amitava Kumar, Marie Myung-Ok Lee, Pooja Makhijani, Dawn Lundy Martin, Michael

Martone, Rahul Mehta, Shaila Mehra, Carley Moore, Michele Morano, Michael Morse, David Mura, Sara Nolan, Minna Proctor, Leslie Roberts, Preeta Samarasan, Robin Beth Schaer, Prageeta Sharma, Sadia Shepherd, Danielle Sosin, Shreerekha Subramanian, and Tanu Mehrotra Wakefield.

Shout out to the women of #HIVEDIT, to the Binders (especially CNF, Memoirists, and Forthcoming), and to the Author's Guild.

I am deeply grateful to the writers whose books made me want to write and which have sustained me over the years I worked on these essays: they include bell hooks, Maxine Hong Kingston, Audre Lorde, Toni Morrison, and Adrienne Rich. I called upon them in troubled times and they helped me gather my resolve and write back.

To my parents, Ashok and Shobhana Shah: your support and encouragement have made my life and creative work possible. Thank you for being lifelong readers and learners who kept me stocked in library books and notebooks. My brother and sister-in-law, Samir Shah and Seema Byahatti: you have always lit the way and had a place for me at your table. Thank you. Anand, I remember your telling me at age six, *No more books, Sejal Foi!*; you were done with that as the default gift. Thanks to you and Vijay for teaching me about cars and planes (KBOS) and showing me the world through your eyes. I feel very lucky to be your aunt.

Thank you to my parents-in-law, Singa and Jambu Singaravelu, for your generosity and kindness. Thank you to my uncle, Kirit N. Shah, the first writer in the family, for your example of reading two newspapers a day, and for always answering my specific and sometimes obscure questions and emails right away. I don't take it for granted. Thank you to my extended family for showing up.

♥

To R: Thank you for everything.

This book is in memory of my maternal grandmother, Indumati Natverlal Shah, and my friend LeeAnne Smith White. They shared a love of beauty, and both had a gift for creating community and joy and for gathering family and friends together. They are in these words, they are in me, and I hope to have invoked them for you, as well.

For my grandparents—I end these words with your names, to honor my ancestors and the work you did and how far you moved from home. I am grateful.

Nathalal Amthalal Shah
Kantaben Nathalal Shah
Natverlal Ambalal Shah
Indumati Natverlal Shah

Notes

I found Margaret Atwood's essay "Nine Beginnings" years ago in *The Writer on Her Work, Volume II: New Essays in New Territory,* edited by Janet Sternberg (New York: Norton, 1992), 150–56. Atwood gave nine different responses to the question "Why do you write?" and through those responses created a powerful, formally inventive essay. I loved the circling and jagged movement and leaps and took the form and question as inspiration for my introduction. Though I later cut the numbers and my introduction is no longer a list essay, what remains are my answers as to why I wrote these essays and this book.

The quoted excerpt from Kakali Bhattacharya comes from her essay "(Un)Settling Imagined Lands: A Par/Des(i) Approach to De/Colonizing Methodologies," in *The Oxford Handbook of Methods for Public Scholarship,* edited by Patricia Leavy (Cambridge: Oxford University Press, 2019), 179–208.

PRELUDE

The title "Prelude" references my favorite dance by the choreographer Garth Fagan, "Prelude: Discipline Is Freedom." I grew up seeing and later studying with Garth Fagan Dance, whose movement vocabulary draws from ballet, American modern dance, and Afro-Caribbean dance. Fagan created his own dance technique and worked almost entirely with dancers of color. His distinctive aesthetic made an impression on me. I saw that you could invent your own language; you just had to train and believe.

સેજલ is my first name in Gujarati. Thank you to my uncle, Kirit N. Shah, for walking me through using Google Translate. The opening of "Prelude" takes as inspiration the title of Noy Holland's *I Was Trying to Describe What It Feels Like: New and Selected Stories* (Berkeley: Counterpoint Press, 2017). The phrase "there is only a door" echoes "it is only a door," a line from Adrienne Rich's "Prospective Immigrants Please Note" (*The Fact of a Door Frame: Poems Selected and New, 1950–1984* [New York: Norton, 1984], 51–52).

"I too call myself I" are the final words of Kamala Das's poem "An Introduction." Thanks to Josna Rege for her long-ago birthday gift of *Nine Indian Women Poets: An Anthology*, edited by Eunice de Souza (Delhi: Delhi University Press, 1997), in which I first discovered the poem. "An Introduction" was originally published in Das's book *Summer in Calcutta* (New Delhi: Rajinder Paul, 1965).

SKIN

"Desi" is a term that means "from the homeland" (homeland = desh) in some South Asian languages. The term "desi" was adopted by progressive South Asian Americans in the nineties. I first heard the term in connection with Desh Pardesh, the multidisciplinary South Asian Arts Festival—activist-literary-creative-queer— in Toronto that ran from 1988 to 2001 (http://www.savac.net /collection/desh-pardesh/). I attended Desh in 1996 and 1998 and met writers, dancers, activists, and musicians I've continued to know through the years. In the late 1990s, I experienced both the term and festival as revolutionary. I wrote "Skin" during a time when the word "desi" felt potent and alive for me. However, I realized while working on this book that I don't use the term anymore and have not in some time—a reader will not find "desi" in my later essays. "Desi" feels dated to me now—of a time or just very specific. First, because it refers only to Indians and not to all South Asians (South Asia as a cultural and political identity: covering several countries, multiple religions and languages, but "desis" would not necessarily include Bangladeshis, Sri Lankans, Nepalis, Pakistanis). Second, because I don't hear it often now where I live in western New York or in the online communities I belong to and at the conferences I attend. In places with larger South Asian American populations, such as New Jersey and the Bay Area, "desi" is certainly still in use.

Network of Indian Professionals (NET-IP) is an organization that started in 1990 and held an annual national conference along with other events and programming. Part of the unstated but understood point of the conference seemed to be about creating opportunities to meet a potential mate. There was a certain generational anxiety in which parents worried about who their children would and did marry—one inevitable, tangible result of the parents' immigration. How would the culture and language and heritage continue if you found a partner who was white or black, "American"? I felt this anxiety, too, when I was in my twenties. I think the fear has subsided as time has gone on, Indian Americans have become more integrated in the larger American culture, and many have married out.

MATRIMONIALS: A TRIPTYCH

I wrote the earliest version of "Matrimonials" in 2002 as the introduction to my MFA thesis, which was a collection of short stories. In revision, I brought the perspectives of 2018, 2019, and intervening years to bear on my earlier essay. Thank you to Jennifer Acker for reading a draft and for comments made a few years ago. I am also grateful to Sergei Lobanov-Rostovsky for reading this essay (and the whole book) and for his suggestions more recently.

For its concise summary of the complex history of Indian immigration to the United States, I drew on the introductory page of the South Asian American Digital Archive (SAADA) website, which is also a terrific resource on the history of South Asians in the United States.

Adrienne Rich's 1984 essay "Invisibility in Academe" provided me with tools to begin to articulate my experiences against the framework and context of academia, and Rich's words have influenced me and so much of my writing. I am grateful for Rich's essay, which has shaped my understanding of power and representation in education and literature. The phrase "real and normative" and the longer excerpt included in the footnote are from page 199 of *Blood, Bread, and Poetry: Selected Prose, 1979–1985* by Adrienne Rich. Copyright © by Adrienne Rich. Used by permission of W. W. Norton & Company. Thank you to Elliot H. Shapiro for introducing me to Rich's prose.

The image of garba dancers described as sea anemones originates in Chitra Banerjee Divakaruni's poem "Garba" in *Black Candle* (Corvallis, OR: Calyx Books, 1991).

The lines from Salman Rushdie's essay "Imaginary Homelands" appear on page 17 of his book of the same name, *Imaginary Homelands: Essays and Criticism, 1981–1991* (New York: Granta, in association with Viking Penguin, 1991).

The poem that I quote from is called "Counting the Ways" and appears on pages 330–31 of *Contours of the Heart: South Asians Map North America*, edited by Sunaina Maira and Rajini Srikanth (New York: Asian American Writers' Workshop, 1996).

Anand Vaishnav's article about matrimonials, "Nice to Meet You. Will You Marry Me?," appeared in the *Boston Globe*, March 30, 2002, on the front page of the Living/Arts section.

WHO'S INDIAN?

My title is a nod to Gish Jen's story collection *Who's Irish?*, in which Jen explores Asian American and Irish American identity. An earlier and slightly different version of "Who's Indian?" appeared under the title "Where Are You From?" in the inaugural issue of *Catamaran: A Magazine of South Asian American Literature* 1 (2003): 21–28. My thanks to the University of Massachusetts at Amherst for a Graduate School Fellowship that supported my travel and to Richard B. Newton (Rick), who led the UMass journalism course and trip to Sicily.

The epigraph to my essay originated in Jasbir K. Puar's important article "Resituating Discourses of 'Whiteness' and 'Asianness' in Northern England: Second Generation Sikh Women and Constructions of Identity," *Socialist Review* 94 (1994): 21–54. I am grateful to Puar for making explicit the assumptions within the question "Where are you from?"

I referenced James Baldwin's essay "Stranger in the Village," about Baldwin's experience living in a remote town in Switzerland in the 1950s, from *Notes of a Native Son* (Boston, MA: Beacon Press, 1955, 1984), 159–75.

I wrote "Who's Indian?" nearly twenty years ago. I am struck by the contrast between the world portrayed in the essay and the current situation of the hundreds of thousands of refugees from the Middle East and North Africa turned away not only from Italy but also from other parts of Europe.

Thank you to my dear friend Ann Gagliardi for sparking my interest in Italy and inviting me to visit her there.

THE WORLD IS FULL OF PAPER. WRITE TO ME.

This essay grew out of remarks I gave at a memorial service for Agha Shahid Ali in 2002 at the University of Massachusetts. I typed up some notes at a common computer in Bartlett Hall and didn't save them but only printed the eulogy. I found my notes a decade later, after many moves between states, while unpacking boxes in my parents' basement. I used my eulogy to write a longer essay about Shahid, published by the Asian American Writers' Workshop's journal, *The Margins*, December 8, 2013, on the twelfth anniversary of his passing and later republished in *Mad Heart Be Brave: Essays on the Poetry of Agha Shahid Ali*, edited by Kazim Ali (Ann Arbor: University of Michigan Press, 2017), 12–19. I took the final two lines of Shahid's poem "Stationery," from *The Half-Inch Himalayas* (Middletown, CT: Wesleyan University Press, 1987), 48, as the title of this essay. Reprinted by permission.

I also quote two lines from Shahid's poem "Farewell," from *The Country without a Post Office* (New York: Norton, 1997), 23. The sentence "I too call myself I" in my postscript is the last line of Kamala Das's poem "An Introduction." I use the same line in "Prelude."

KINSHIP, COUSINS, & KHICHIDI

I wish to thank Kirit N. Shah for emailing me the standard diacritical transliterations of several Gujarati words that appear in this essay, even though I decided not to use all of his suggestions. The transliterations in the essay are a combination—of standard and what looked right to my eyes.

When I read Geeta Kothari's essay "If You Are What You Eat, Then What Am I?," I admired the segmented form she used. Reading her essay inspired my own. Kothari's piece appeared in the *Kenyon Review* 21 (1999): 6–14, and was later republished in *Best American Essays 2000*, edited by Alan Lightman (Boston, MA: Houghton Mifflin, 2000), 91–100, which is where I read it. Thank you to Anita Mannur for inviting me to submit work to the special issue on food of the *Massachusetts Review* she guest edited in 2004; I wrote my essay in response to her call.

STREET SCENE

Maurice Utrillo's painting *Street Scene* inspired this essay. The painting belongs to the permanent collection of the University of Rochester's museum, the Memorial Art Gallery, in Rochester, New York. Thank you to Joanna Scott of the University of Rochester for welcoming me into her Sense of Place course while I was on sabbatical from teaching at Marymount Manhattan College. This essay, as well as "Bird" and "Walking Tributaries," began as writing for assignments for her class. I am grateful to Mount Holyoke College, where I taught in 2003–2004; my faculty research funds made this trip to Paris possible in 2004.

BIRD

The idea that each relationship is its own animal with its own life and memory came from Abigail Thomas's memoir *Safekeeping: Some True Stories from a Life* (New York: Anchor Books, 2000), 141. The idea and image stayed with me, as has her book.

WALKING TRIBUTARIES

Thank you to Jane Hawley, Luther College professor of dance, for inviting me to collaborate with her in the summer of 2008. I am grateful to Marymount Manhattan College for funding this work, to Sandhya and Brian Caton for hosting me, and to Amanda Hamp for further collaboration. Leigh Wheaton, one of the dancers in the collaborative, read my poem "Independence, Iowa," which was later published in *Indivisible: An Anthology of Contemporary South Asian American Poetry*, edited by Neelanjana Banerjee, Summi Kaipa, and Pireeni Sundaralingam (Fayetteville: University of Arkansas Press, 2010), 64–65. The lines I quote by Luther College English professor David Faldet are from *Oneota Flow: The Upper Iowa River and Its People* (Iowa City: University of Iowa Press, 2009), 4. Thank you to the University of Iowa Press for permission to reprint this excerpt.

I quote Toni Morrison from her essay/speech "The Site of Memory," which I first read in *Out There: Marginalization and Contemporary Cultures*, edited by Russell Ferguson, Martha Gever, Trinh T. Minh-ha, and Cornel West (New York: New Museum of Contemporary Art and Massachusetts Institute of Technology,

1990), 299–305, excerpt on page 305. I gratefully acknowledge the late Toni Morrison and ICM Partners for permission to reprint this excerpt.

CASTLE, FORT, LOOKOUT, HOUSE

This essay grew out of a prompt given by Abigail Thomas in her writing workshop at the Ninety-Second Street Y in Tribeca: "It was not X I wanted, it was Y. However, I got an X." Thomas credited inspiration for the prompt to the opening lines of Brigit Pegeen Kelley's poem "Iskandariya."

I adapted my definitions of "quarry" from several I found online, including in the *Oxford English Dictionary* and on Wikipedia in 2011.

YOUR WILDERNESS IS NOT PERMANENT

"The Love of My Life," by Cheryl Strayed, appeared in the September 2002 issue of *The Sun*. I am grateful to editors Bradford Morrow and Nicole Nyhan at *Conjunctions*, where this essay first appeared, for making what I had written better and catching what I missed. Thank you to Aviva Grossberg, Christian Nagler, and Anne Mavromatis.

THERE IS NO MIKE HERE

"There Is No Mike Here" was originally published in the Asian American Writers' Workshop online journal, *The Margins*, in "After Yi-Fen Chou: A Forum—19 Writers Respond to Michael Derrick Hudson's Yellowface," on September 15, 2015. The introduction to the folio states, "Early last week, news broke that Yi-Fen Chou, whose poem is included in *The Best American Poetry 2015*, is not a Chinese poet, but in fact is a white man named Michael Derrick Hudson. After little success submitting poems under his real name, Hudson decided to take on the Chinese name Yi-Fen Chou—a name, it turns out, shared by a high school classmate of his. His poem was accepted by the journal *Prairie Schooner* and later chosen by Sherman Alexie for this year's anthology of *Best American Poetry*.... We asked writers within the AAWW community to send us their responses to Michael Derrick Hudson's yellowface."

Also included in this introduction was the following excerpt from a piece Ken Chen, former executive director of AAWW, wrote for NPR Code Switch: "American literature isn't just an art form—it's a segregated labor market. In New York, where almost 70 percent of New Yorkers are people of color, all but 5 percent of writers reviewed in the *New York Times* are white. Hudson saw these crumbs and asked why they weren't his. Rather than being a savvy opportunist, he's another hysterical white man, envious of the few people of color who've breached their quarantine" ("Why a White Poet Posed as Asian to Get Published, and What's Wrong with That," *All Things Considered*, September 10, 2015).

In 2018, three years after I wrote my essay, Sherman Alexie's harassment of women writers surfaced in the news. I taught Alexie's story "What You Pawn I Will Redeem," collected in *Best American Short Stories 2004*, edited by Lorrie Moore (Boston, MA: Houghton Mifflin, 2004) 1–21 and originally published in the April 21 and April 28, 2003, issue of the *New Yorker*, for a long time. I don't know if I will teach it again. I could say the same thing about a few other writers. I did not cut them out of my work, finally (their writing has influenced my own), but I thought hard about whether or not to allot them space in my book. That lineage is still there, but I chose to reduce some of the space.

The story about Thanksgiving that I mention, "Giving Is Thanks" by Amy Morris Lillie, is included in the textbook *Paths to Follow*, edited by Ullin W. Leavell, Mary Louise Friebele, and Tracie Cushman (New York: American Book Company, 1956), 262–67.

I stumbled on Angela Jackson's poem "The Love of Travelers" in *The Pushcart Prize, XIV*, edited by Bill Henderson (New York:

Penguin Books, 1989). The excerpt quoted comes from page 232 of this anthology. "The Love of Travelers" is copyrighted in 1998 by Jackson, in *And All These Roads Be Luminous: Poems Selected and New* (Evanston, IL: *TriQuarterly*/Northwestern University Press, 1998).

TEMPORARY TALISMANS

My short story "The Girl with Two Brothers" first appeared in *Denver Quarterly* 45, no. 1 (2010): 80–87. The excerpts from Christian McEwen's *World Enough and Time: On Creativity and Slowing Down* (Peterborough, NH: Bauhan Publishing, 2011) are taken from pages 172–73.

SIX HOURS FROM ANYWHERE YOU WANT TO BE

In this essay I included my description of western New York as "disturbingly close to Ohio," taken from my short story "The Half King," which appeared in the scenester issue of *The Literary Review* 56, no. 2 (early summer 2013): 23–37. The quotation "The world is divided between those who stay and those who leave" is taken from Bharati Mukherjee's novel *Jasmine* (New York: Grove Weidenfeld, 1989), 228. The poem "Stay Home," copyright © 2012 by Wendell Berry, is from *New Collected Poems* and reprinted by permission of Counterpoint Press.

SARIS AND SORROWS

Thank you to Scott Seifritz for the opportunity to read a draft of this essay at his Speakeasy reading series, and to Jacob Rakovan for his smart, insightful feedback after the reading.

During our three-hour wedding ceremony on June 26, 2015, the U.S. Supreme Court legalized gay marriage. Making the legal and social benefits of marriage more accessible to all felt momentous and helped mitigate my ambivalence about having such a traditional (and not even in my tradition!) and patriarchal ceremony.

I am grateful to have found a person I wanted to make a life with, and fortunate to have had a meaningful celebration. However, getting married is not the prize. I had been single for a long time, and I had been happy (and unhappy) in that life, too. Not everyone wants to get married. And there are many reasons to dance.

'

CPSIA information can be obtained
at www.ICGtesting.com
Printed in the USA
LVHW090213190921
698068LV00006B/7

9 780820 357232